THE
AMERICAN
STREAMLINER
POSTWAR YEARS

Dieselized City of Portland, *a premier Union Pacific train, glides through the grandeur of the Columbia River Gorge in Oregon. Union Pacific*

Following an initial press run from Chicago to French Lick, Indiana, and return on the Monon, the blue and silver Train of Tomorrow *departed on an exhibition tour of Eastern cities in the summer of 1947. The train, the idea for which was originated by General Motors in 1944, included four Astra Dome cars and featured a 2,000-hp E-7 diesel, a chair car, sleeper, diner and an observation-lounge car. The train featured air conditioning, anti-friction bearings and fluorescent lighting. Two-way radio-telephone equipment was also installed on the train, and all windows, including those in the dome cars, were glazed with special Thermopane, consisting of two panes of glass separated by a dehydrated air space hermetically sealed in at the glass factory by a metal-to-glass bond. Here the train poses with some original, early Baltimore & Ohio passenger equipment. "Some day, perhaps sooner than you think, its (the train's) revolutionary advances in comfort and convenience will begin to appear in regularly scheduled trains," read a promotion brochure for the train.*

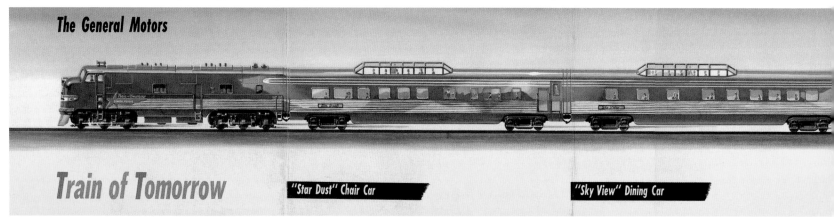

The General Motors

Train of Tomorrow   "Star Dust" Chair Car   "Sky View" Dining Car

The idea was born, and sketches quickly reached the GM styling section in Detroit. Soon engineering analysis was being undertaken at Pullman-Standard in response to GM's request. At war's end in 1945, EMD placed an order with Pullman-Standard for a 4-car *Train of Tomorrow* which gave 216 patrons the latest and finest features of postwar streamliner travel. All four cars—coach, diner, sleeper and observation—were domes.

Naturally, EMD's new E-7 passenger diesel provided road power, but not so well known is the fact that five other GM divisions participated in the venture. The Styling Section handled the interior design, Frigidare Division was responsible for the air conditioning and refrigeration systems, Detroit Diesel Division and Delco Products Division designed separate diesel-electric generators for individual car power and the Hyatt Bearing Division provided the roller bearings on the locomotive—like outside bearing swing hanger trucks.

When the *Train of Tomorrow* was finally completed by Pullman-Standard, GM had a memorable pre-inaugural invitation-only run between Chicago and French Lick, Indiana on May 26-27, 1947. The following day, the formal debut commenced with a banquet at Chicago's Palmer House for 1,000 business and civic leaders at GM's expense. The train was then sent on a nationwide tour.

For 65,000 miles from the Burlington to the Boston & Maine, and Portland, Oregon to Portland, Maine, crowds flocked by the thousands to see the new train. The streamliner was on public display at the 1948 and 1949 Chicago Railroad

"n Cloud" Sleeping Car   "Moon Glow" Observation Car

fairs. In 1950, the train joined the Union Pacific fleet and became its contribution to Union Pacific/Great Northern/Northern Pacific Portland-Seattle pool service for over a decade.

Proud as GM/Pullman was of the *Train of Tomorrow*, it did not contain the first true dome. Streamliner promoter and Burlington President Ralph Budd saw to that. Aware of the GM/Pullman project, Budd instructed his own shops at Aurora, Illinois to rebuild stainless steel coach *Silver Alchemy* with "something different" added.

After much consultation between Budd and Burlington's engineering and mechanical forces, in June, 1945 the coach-turned-dome named *Silver Dome* emerged. For structural reasons it did not contain a depressed floor under the dome

area but was an instant major hit regardless. The Burlington responded by placing an order for 40 dome coaches with Budd for Twin Cities, Denver and various other *Zephyr* services.

Thus began a railroad hallmark which ultimately totalled but 235 cars. A clear majority were built by Budd, but Pullman-Standard and American Car & Foundry were well represented. All were memorable railroading and engineering accomplishments, whether in coach, diner, sleeper or observation format.

Vertical clearance permitting, the majority of streamliners included at least one Vista-Dome, Astra-Dome, Strata-Dome, Planetarium-Dome, or perhaps most telling of all, simply Pleasure Dome car.

This dramatic night shot of CB&Q's Silver Garden *dome-coach-buffet-lounge in December of 1952 testifies to the promotions the railroads used to publicize their streamlined trains. This car was used on the* Kansas City Zephyr. Budd

The Denver Zephyr *vista dome interior was comfortable, with plenty of windows for passengers to view the passing landscape. Budd*

8—Cincinnati Union Terminal at Night, Cincinnati, Ohio

3A-H934

Cincinnati Union Terminal at night was a beautiful structure. Still standing, the station in the mid-forties was used by the Chesapeake & Ohio, the Baltimore & Ohio, Louisville & Nashville, New York Central, Norfolk & Western, Pennsylvania and Southern.

A 2,000-hp diesel powered the Rock Island's Peoria Rocket, *daily trains #501 and 503, which featured reserved seating but not extra fares. The Chicago to Peoria run featured a 14-section sleeping car, but neither train would handle corpses.*

The Rock Island's Rocket *slides through Minneapolis with two diesels and a short consist in June of 1952. Russ Porter*

Cover of the February, 1953 Rock Island timetable still displayed diesel and steam power, but steam was waning. Inside, the promotional copy read, "All Rock Island 'Rockets' conform to the same high standards—diesel power—modern equipment—timely schedules and courteous service."

FIRST FLOWERINGS: THE POSTWAR SCRAMBLE

Regardless of how many new diesels and passenger cars any individual railroad could afford to purchase, until delivery came, they were but so much advertising hype. Using various juggling acts, many roads stretched their existing prewar equipment to the absolute limit.

The revitalized Rock Island actually led the postwar scramble by more than 15 months. On January 15, 1945 it placed a new streamliner, the *Twin Star Rocket*, in service between Minneapolis-St.Paul and Houston, Texas. No new equipment could be acquired for the service, thus the RI was forced to swap around existing equipment

Rock Island 2,000-hp DL-109 Alco #621 was one of only four Alco RI passenger engines to wear Rocket dress. It was delivered to the railroad in October of 1941, and survived in passenger service to the end of l967. Along with its three sisters, Nos. 622-624, the locomotives were unique in styling and #621 became the sole example of an EMD-repowered DL-109 before its demise.

After World War II, even the major coal hauling railroads such as the Norfolk & Western, which used steam power up until the very end, streamlined their coal-consuming locomotives. Here the Pocahontas, *a fast overnight train between east-west end points Norfolk and Cincinnati, featuring luxury sleepers and superior dining car service, heads down the main line.*

The Pocahontas, on Norfolk and Western R. R.

PHOTOGRAPH BY NORFOLK & WESTERN RAILWAY   2B-H534

TOP. *The N&W streamlined J Class passenger locomotive was a 4-8-4 with 80,000 pounds of tractive effort and an additional 12,500 pounds from a booster. The driving wheels were 70 inches. BELOW. In action, the J was an impressive locomotive: the boiler measured 61 feet in length, with an additional 47 feet for the 20,000-gallon tender.*

Norfolk & Western was the first railroad to inaugurate new postwar passenger service. Using streamlined Class J locomotives, the railroad built a reputation of comfort, congeniality and courtesy.

to create the necessary three train sets.

First after V-J Day was the Norfolk & Western. On April 26, 1946 it inaugurated streamliner service between Cincinnati, Ohio and Norfolk, Virginia. Using pre-war equipment and streamlined 4-8-4 steam locomotives, two 7-car coach *Powhatan Arrows* were placed on line. It was the first new postwar service actually inaugurated.

Several weeks later, on June 2, 1946, the Southern Pacific rearranged existing equipment in its

pool to form the new *Sacramento Daylight* to extend the existing *San Joaquin Daylight* to California's capital city.

Simultaneously, the Union Pacific and Wabash premiered service from St. Louis to the West as the *City of St. Louis*. All the equipment was from existing UP secondary trains, including the *Challenger*. Service was on the Wabash between St. Louis and Kansas City. Connection into the UP main was at Cheyenne, with coaches and sleepers direct to Portland, San Francisco or Los Angeles.

An early EMD-built Wabash passenger E unit features a Mars light at the top of the nose; later models featured numberboards below the two small nose lights. The Wabash, basically a bridge line, first saw diesels in 1946 which were used in pool service with the Union Pacific pulling the City of St. Louis *and the* City of Kansas City *between Denver and St. Louis. By 1953 the entire line was dieselized, except for a couple of ancient 2-6-0s on the Bluffs-Keokuk branch.*

American Car & Foundry of St. Louis was a major player in the passenger car building frenzy of the postwar period. In November of 1947 it delivered this diner-lounge car to the Wabash Railroad. Car #50 seated 54 passengers.

Santa Fe had its own immediate postwar improvements planned for the warbonnet fleet. In September, 1946 the *Super Chief* and *El Capitan* began every-other-day service. Even days saw *Super Chief* service; odd days saw *El Capitan* service. Building on its association with Indian heritage, the Santa Fe also added Zuni or Navajo Indian guides to its trains as they passed through the Southwest, which proved an instant hit.

Fully committed to dieselization, the Santa Fe ordered EMD's new 1,500-hp F-3 locomotive and the first of competitor Alco/GE's new 2,000-hp PA, both for passenger work. If anything wore warbonnet paint better than an F unit, it was the PA. Santa Fe matched them against the F's, and while the PA's won the styling contest, the pulling contest belonged to the F's. Santa Fe ultimately purchased F's by the hundreds, but only 44 PA's.

MICHIGAN FIRST: THE *PERE MARQUETTE*

While all of America's major railroads clamored for hurry-up delivery of their new streamliners, a small Midwestern road actually placed the first postwar streamliner of all-new construction into revenue service.

On August 10, 1946 the C&O-controlled Pere Marquette inaugurated two 7-car streamliners of the same name between Detroit and Grand Rapids, Michigan via Lansing. The 152-mile route was scheduled for 2 hours, 40 minutes, and the two equipment sets provided a total of three daily roundtrips. Each set consisted of an EMD 2,000-hp E-7 locomotive, baggage car, mail car, two coach-lounges, two coach-observations and diner. All cars were built by Pullman-Standard and painted with a yellow letterboard, blue window stripe and stainless steel lower side panels.

Interior design included colors of tan and green, with contrast provided by the carpeting, drapes and seating. Each coach seated 54, with nine additional seats in the smoking lounge. The coach-observations seated 56, plus 10 observation seats.

Another feature of the *Pere Marquette* was the first use of Heywood-Wakefield Company's new Sleepy Hollow coach seats. Developed by Dr. Ernest Hooton of Harvard University, nearly 4,000 people were measured in Boston's North Station to determine the best specifications for the most comfortable seat for the average person. An

Page Seven

Name of Train	Road(s) on which Operated	Between	Equipment	Power
City of Los Angeles	C&NW;UP	Chicago-Los Angeles	Streamline	Diesel-Electric
City of Memphis	NC&StL	Nashville-Memphis	"	Steam
City of Miami	IC;CofGa;ACL;FEC	Chicago-Miami	"	Diesel-Electric
City of Milwaukee "400"	C&NW	Chicago-Milwaukee	"	" "
City of New Orleans	IC	Chicago-St. Louis-Louisville-New Orleans	"	" "
City of Portland	C&NW;UP	Chicago-Portland	"	" "
City of St. Louis	Wabash;UP	St. Louis-Kansas City-Denver	"	" "
City of San Francisco	C&NW;UP;SP	Chicago-San Francisco	"	" "
Cleveland-Chicago Express	NYC	Cleveland to Chicago	Standard	Steam
Cleveland-Cincinnati Night Special	NYC	St. Louis to Cincinnati & Cleveland	"	"
Cleveland-Cincinnati Special	NYC	Cleveland to Cincinnati	"	"
Cleveland Express (No. 420)	NYC	Indianapolis to Cleveland	"	"
Cleveland Express (No. 444)	NYC	Columbus to Cleveland	"	"
Cleveland Limited	NYC	New York-Cleveland	"	Electric; Steam
Cleveland Mail	NYC	Toronto & Buffalo to Cleveland	"	Steam
Cleveland Night Express	B&O	Cleveland-Washington-Baltimore	"	"
Cleveland-St. Louis Special	NYC	Cleveland to St. Louis	"	"
Cleveland Special	NYC	Cincinnati to Cleveland	"	"
Clevelander, The	PRR	New York-Washington-Cleveland	"	Electric; D-E
Coast Line Florida Mail	RF&P;ACL	(See Florida Mail)		
Coaster	SP	San Francisco-Los Angeles	"	Steam
Colonial, The	NYNH&H;PRR	Boston-New York-Washington	"	D-E; Electric
Colorado Eagle	MP;D&RGW	St. Louis-Kansas City-Pueblo-Denver	Streamline	Diesel-Electric
Colorado Express	CRI&P	Kansas City-Denver	Standard	Steam

Page Seven

Page Eight

Name of Train	Road(s) on which Operated	Between	Equipment	Power
Columbia River Express	SP&S	Pasco-Portland	Standard	Steam
Columbian	CMStP&P	Chicago-Minneapolis-Butte-Spokane-Seattle-Tacoma	"	Steam; Electric
Columbian, The	B&O	Washington-Chicago	Streamline	Diesel-Electric
Columbine, The	UP	Omaha-Denver	Standard	Steam
Columbus-Cincinnati Special	NYC	Cleveland to Cincinnati	"	"
Comet, The	NYNH&H	Cohasset-Braintree-Whitman	Streamline	Diesel-Electric
Commander, The	NYNH&H	Boston-New York	Standard	D-E or Steam; Elect.
Commodore Vanderbilt, The	NYC	New York-Chicago	"	Electric; Diesel-Electric
Commuter "400"	C&NW	Chicago-Milwaukee	Streamline	Electric
Congressional, The	PRR	New York-Washington	Standard	Electric
Connecticut Yankee	NYNH&H;B&M;CV;CP	New York-Boston-White River Junction-Quebec	"	Electric; Diesel-Electric; Steam
Constitution, The	PRR	New York-Washington	"	Electric
Continental Limited, The (Trains 1 & 2)	CN	Montreal-Ottawa-Winnipeg-Jasper-Vancouver	"	Steam
Continental Limited, The (Trains 3 & 4)	CN	Toronto-Winnipeg-Jasper-Vancouver	"	"
Copper Country Limited	CMStP&P;DSS&A*	Chicago-Milwaukee-Sault Ste. Marie-Calumet	"	"
Corn Belt Rocket	CRI&P	Chicago-Omaha	Streamline	Diesel-Electric
Cotton Blossom, The	RF&P;SAL	Washington-Atlanta-Birmingham	Standard	Steam; D-E
Cracker, The	Southern	Atlanta-Macon-Brunswick	Unit	Diesel-Electric
Crescent, The	PRR;Southern;A&WP;WofAla;L&N	New York-Washington-Atlanta-New Orleans	Standard	Electric; Diesel-Electric; Steam

Page Eight

Page Nine

Name of Train	Road(s) on which Operated	Between	Equipment	Power
*Crusader, The	Reading;CofNJ	Philadelphia-New York	Streamline	Steam

D

Name of Train	Road(s) on which Operated	Between	Equipment	Power
Dakotan	GN	St. Paul-Williston, N.D.	Standard	Steam
Day Cape Codder (s)	NYNH&H	New York-Woods Hole & Hyannis	"	Electric; D-E
Day Express	CI&L	Chicago-Louisville	"	Steam
Day White Mountains	NYNH&H;B&M;CV;CN	New York-Woodsville-Berlin, N.H.-Montreal	"	Electric; D-E or Steam
Daylight	SP	(See Morning Daylight and Noon Daylight)		
Daylight, The	IC	Chicago-St. Louis	Streamline	Diesel-Electric
Daylight Express	FEC	Jacksonville-Miami	Standard	Steam
Del-Mar-Va Express	PRR	New York-Cape Charles	"	Electric; Steam
Del Monte	SP	San Francisco-Pacific Grove	"	Steam
Delta Eagle, The	MP	Memphis-Helena-Tallulah	Streamline	Diesel-Electric
Denver Zephyr	CB&Q	Chicago-Denver	"	"
Des Moines-Chicago Rocket	CRI&P	Des Moines-Chicago	"	" "
Des Moines Limited	Wabash	St. Louis to Des Moines	Standard	Steam
Des Moines-Omaha Limited	CRI&P	Chicago-Des Moines-Omaha	"	"
Detroit Arrow, The	PRR; Wabash	Chicago to Detroit	"	"
Detroit Limited	Wabash	St. Louis to Detroit	"	"
Detroit Special	NYC	Chicago-Detroit	"	"
Detroit Special	Wabash	St. Louis to Detroit	"	"
Detroiter, The	NYC	New York-Detroit	"	Electric; Steam
DeWitt Clinton	NYC	Buffalo to New York	"	Steam; Electric

*Two round trips weekdays.

Page Nine

Page Ten

Name of Train	Road(s) on which Operated	Between	Equipment	Power
Diplomat, The	B&O;Reading;CofNJ	St. Louis-Washington-New York	Standard	Diesel-Electric
Dixie Flagler	C&EI;L&N;NC&StL;ACL;FEC	Chicago-Miami	Streamline	Steam; D-E
Dixie Flyer	C&EI;L&N;NC&StL;CofGa;ACL;FEC	Chicago-Jacksonville-Miami-Tampa-St. Petersburg	Standard	Steam
Dixie Limited	C&EI;L&N;NC&StL;CofGa;ACL;FEC	Chicago-Atlanta-Jacksonville-Orlando-Miami	"	"
Dixie Mail	C&EI;L&N	Chicago-Evansville-Nashville	"	"
Dixieland, The (w)	C&EI;L&N;NC&StL;ACL;FEC	Chicago-Nashville-Jacksonville-Miami	"	Steam; D-E
Dominion, The	CP	Montreal-Toronto-Vancouver	"	Steam
Dominion Express	PRR	Washington-Philadelphia-Buffalo	"	Electric; Steam
Down Easter (s)	NYNH&H;B&M;MeC	New York-Plymouth, N.H.-Rockland-Waterville, Me.	"	Electric; Diesel-Electric; Steam
Duluth-Superior Limited	C&NW	Chicago to Duluth	"	Steam
Duquesne, The	PRR	New York-Pittsburgh	"	Electric; Steam

E

Name of Train	Road(s) on which Operated	Between	Equipment	Power
East Coast Express (w)	FEC	Jacksonville-Miami	Standard	Steam
Easterner, The	NYC	Toledo to Buffalo & New York	"	Steam; Electric
East Wind (s)	NYNH&H;B&M	New York-Portland	"	Electric; Steam or Diesel-Electric

Page Ten

Page Eleven

Name of Train	Road(s) on which Operated	Between	Equipment	Power
*Eastern Slope (w)	B&M	Boston-North Conway-Intervale	Standard	Steam
Edison, The	PRR	New York-Washington	"	Electric
Egyptian, The	NYC	Chicago-Harrisburg, Ill.	"	Steam
El Capitan	Santa Fe	Chicago-Los Angeles	Streamline	Diesel-Electric
El Dorado	SP	San Francisco-Sacramento	Standard	Steam
El Rapido	NdeM	(See Sunshine Special;MP)		
Embassy, The	PRR	New York-Washington		Electric
Empire Builder, The	CB&Q;GN;SP&S	Chicago-Seattle-Portland	Streamline	D-E; Electric
Empire Express	P&LE;NYC	Pittsburgh-Buffalo	Standard	Steam
Empire State Express	NYC	New York-Buffalo-Cleveland-Detroit	"	Electric; Steam
Erie Limited, The	Erie	New York-Buffalo-Chicago	"	Diesel-Electric
Essex Special (s)	CofNJ	Newark to Bay Head Junction	"	Steam
Everglades	RF&P;ACL	Washington-Jacksonville	"	Steam; D-E
Executive, The	PRR	New York-Washington	"	Electric
Exposition Flyer, The	CB&Q;D&RGW;WP	Chicago-San Francisco	"	Diesel-Electric

F

Name of Train	Road(s) on which Operated	Between	Equipment	Power
Fast Fifteen	Santa Fe	Newton, Kans., to Galveston	Standard	Steam
F.F.V., The (The Fast Flying Virginian)	PRR;C&O	New York-Washington Norfolk-Cincinnati-Louisville	"	Electric; Steam
Fast Mail	C&NW	Eau Claire, Wis.-Duluth, Min.	"	Steam
Fast Mail	CB&Q	Chicago-Omaha-Lincoln	"	Diesel-Electric
Fast Mail	GN	St. Paul-Minneapolis-Seattle	"	D-E; Steam

*Week-end snow train.

Page Eleven

Page Twelve

Name of Train	Road(s) on which Operated	Between	Equipment	Power
Fast Mail, The	CMStP&P	Minneapolis & St. Paul to Milwaukee & Chicago	Standard	Diesel-Electric
Fast Mail Express	Santa Fe	Chicago-Los Angeles	"	Steam
Feather River Express	WP	San Francisco-Portola	"	Steam; Electric
Federal, The	NYNH&H; PRR	Boston-New York-Washington	"	D-E; Electric
Fifth Avenue Special	NYC	Chicago & Toledo to New York	"	Steam; Electric
Firefly, The	StLSF	Oklahoma City-Tulsa-Kansas City	Streamline	Steam
Fisherman, The (s)	CMStP&P	Chicago-Wausau-Woodruff-Minocqua	Standard	Steam; D-E
Fisherman's Special (s)	PRSL	Philadelphia-Cape May Harbor	"	Steam
Flambeau, The (s)	C&NW	Chicago-Watersmeet-Ironwood	"	"
Flamingo, The	L&N;CofGa;ACL;FEC	Cincinnati-Louisville-Atlanta-Jacksonville-Miami	"	Steam; D-E
Florida Arrow, The (w)	PRR;L&N;ACL;FEC	Chicago-Louisville-Jacksonville-Miami	"	" " "
Florida Mail	RF&P;ACL	Washington-Jacksonville	"	" " "
Florida Special (New York Section)(w)	PRR;RF&P;ACL;FEC	New York-Washington-Miami	"	Electric; Steam; Diesel-Electric
Florida Special (Washington Section)(w)	RF&P;ACL;FEC	Washington-Miami-Tampa-St. Petersburg	"	Steam; D-E
Florida Sunbeam, The (w)	NYC;Southern;SAL	Chicago-Detroit-Cleveland-Cincinnati-Miami	"	" " "
Flying Crow, The	KCS;L&A	Kansas City-Shreveport-Port Arthur-New Orleans	"	Diesel-Electric
Flying Yankee	B&M;MeC	Boston-Portland-Bangor	"	" "
Forest City, The	NYC	Cleveland to Detroit & Chicago	"	Steam

Page Twelve

Name of Train	Road(s) on which Operated	Between	Equipment	Power
Fort Hayes, The	PRR	Chicago-Columbus	Standard	Steam
Fort Pitt, The	PRR	Chicago to Pittsburg	"	"
Forty-Second Street Express	NYNH&H	Boston to New York	"	D-E; Electric
Frontenac, The	CP	Montreal-Quebec	"	Steam
G				
Gateway, The	NYC	Buffalo & Cleveland to St. Louis	Standard	Steam
General, The	PRR	New York-Chicago	Streamline	Electric; D-E
General Pershing Zephyr	CB&Q	St. Louis-Kansas City	"	Diesel-Electric
Genesee, The	NYC	New York-Buffalo	Standard	Electric; Steam
George Washington, The	PRR;C&O;NYC;MP;T&P	New York-Washington-Norfolk-Cincinnati-Louisville-Chicago-St. Louis-San Antonio	"	Electric; Steam; Diesel-Electric
Georgian, The	L&N;NC&StL	St. Louis-Evansville-Nashville-Atlanta	Streamline	Diesel-Electric
Gilt Edge, The	NYNH&H	New York-Boston	"	Electric; D-E
Gold Coast, The	C&NW;UP;SP	Chicago-Omaha-San Francisco	Standard	Steam
*Golden Gate	Santa Fe	Bakersfield-Oakland	Streamline	Diesel-Electric
Golden State, The	CRI&P;SP	Chicago-Los Angeles	"	"
Golden Triangle, The	PRR	Chicago-Pittsburgh	Standard	Steam
Goldenrod, The	Southern	Birmingham-Mobile	Unit	Diesel-Electric
Gopher, The	GN	St. Paul-Minneapolis-Superior-Duluth	Standard	
Gotham Limited, The	PRR	Chicago to New York	"	D-E; Electric
Governor, The	SP	San Francisco-Sacramento	"	Steam
Governor, The	PRR	Philadelphia-Harrisburg	"	Electric

*Two round trips daily.

Name of Train	Road(s) on which Operated	Between	Equipment	Power
Grand Canyon, The	Santa Fe	Chicago-Grand Canyon-Los Angeles-Oakland	Streamline	Diesel-Electric
Great Lakes Limited	B&O	Detroit-Cincinnati-Louisville	Standard	Steam
Great West	CP	Winnipeg-Edmonton	"	"
Green Diamond, The	IC	Chicago-St. Louis	Streamline	Diesel-Electric
Green Mountain, The	NYC;B&M;Rutland;CN	New York-Boston-Montreal	Standard	Electric; Steam; Diesel-Electric
Gulf Coast Rebel	GM&O	St. Louis-Montgomery-Mobile	Streamline	Diesel-Electric
Gulf Coast Special, The	C&S;FW&DC	Denver-Dallas	Standard	Steam
Gulf Stream	FEC	Jacksonville-Miami	"	Diesel-Electric
Gull	B&M;MeC;CP;CN	Boston-Saint John-Halifax	"	D-E; Steam
H				
Hampton Express	LI	New York-Montauk	Standard	Electric; Steam
Harrisburg Special	CofNJ;CofPa;Reading	New York-Harrisburg	"	Steam
Havana Special	PRR;RF&P;ACL;FEC	New York-Washington-Miami-Tampa-St. Petersburg	"	Electric; Steam; Diesel-Electric
Hawkeye, The	IC	Chicago-Sioux City	"	Steam
Hell Gate Express	NYNH&H	New York-Boston	"	Electric; D-E
Henry M. Flagler	FEC	(See Dixie Flagler)		
Hiawatha	CMStP&P	(See Morning Hiawatha and Afternoon Hiawatha)		
Hiawatha (North Woods Service)	CMStP&P	Chicago-Wausau-Woodruff-Minocqua	Streamline	Steam; D-E

Name of Train	Road(s) on which Operated	Between	Equipment	Power
Highlander, The (s)	CN	Toronto-Haliburton	Standard	Steam
Hoosier, The	CI&L	Chicago-Indianapolis-West Baden-French Lick-Louisville	"	"
Hot Springs Limited	CRI&P	Hot Springs-Memphis	"	"
Hot Springs Special	MP	St. Louis-Little Rock-Hot Springs	"	"
Housatonic Express (s)	NYNH&H	New York-Pittsfield	"	Electric; Steam
Houstonian, The	MP	New Orleans-Houston	"	Steam
Hub, The	NYNH&H	New York-Boston	"	Elect; D-E or Steam
Hudson River Express	NYC	Albany to New York	"	Steam; Electric
Hummer, The	GM&O	Chicago-Kansas City	"	Diesel-Electric
Humming Bird, The	L&N	Cincinnati-Louisville-Birmingham-New Orleans	Streamline	"
Hunterdon Hills Express	CofNJ	New York-Hampton	Standard	Steam
Hustler, The	SP	Houston-Dallas	Streamline	"
I				
Idahoan (See also Pony Express)	UP	Salt Lake City-Pocatello-Spokane	Standard	Steam
Illini	IC	Chicago-Carbondale	"	"
Illmo Limited, The	Ill.Term.	Peoria-St. Louis	"	Electric
Imperial, The	CRI&P;SP	Chicago-Los Angeles	"	D-E; Steam
Indianapolis Express	NYC	Detroit to Indianapolis & St. Louis	"	Steam
Inter-City Limited, The	CN;GTW	Montreal-Toronto-Detroit-Port Huron-Chicago	"	"
International Limited, The	CN;GTW	Montreal-Toronto-Port Huron-Chicago	"	"
Interstate Express	NYC	Chicago-Buffalo-Boston	"	"

Name of Train	Road(s) on which Operated	Between	Equipment	Power
Interstate Express	Reading;CofPa;DL&W	Philadelphia-Binghamton-Syracuse	Standard	Steam
Iowan, The	IC	Chicago-Sioux City	"	"
Iron and Copper Country Express	C&NW	Chicago-Ishpeming	"	"
Iron City Express	PRR	New York-Washington-Pittsburgh	"	Electric; Steam
Iroquois, The	NYC	New York & Boston to Chicago	"	Steam
Irvin S. Cobb	IC	Louisville-Memphis	"	"
J				
James Whitcomb Riley	NYC	Chicago to Indianapolis & Cincinnati	Streamline	Steam
Jeffersonian, The	PRR	New York-Washington-St. Louis	"	Electric; D-E
John Wilkes, The	LV	New York-Wilkes Barre-Coxton	"	"
Judiciary, The	PRR	New York-Washington	Standard	Electric
Juniata, The	PRR	Pittsburgh to New York	"	Steam; Electric
K				
Kansas City-Florida Special	StLSF;Southern;FEC	Kansas City-Birmingham-Atlanta-Jacksonville-Miami	Standard	Steam
Kansas Cityan, The	Santa Fe	Chicago to Kansas City & Oklahoma City	Streamline	Diesel-Electric
Katy Flyer	MKT	St. Louis-Kansas City-Oklahoma City-San Antonio-Houston	Standard	Steam
Katy Limited	MKT	Kansas City-Dallas-Ft. Worth-San Antonio	"	"
Kennebec	B&M;MeC	Boston-Portland-Bangor	"	Diesel-Electric
Kentuckian, The	PRR	Chicago-Louisville	"	Steam

Name of Train	Road(s) on which Operated	Between	Equipment	Power
Kettle Valley Express	CP	Vancouver to Medicine Hat	Standard	Steam
Keystone Express	DL&W	Pittsburgh to Scranton	"	"
Klamath	SP	San Francisco-Portland	"	Electric; Steam
Knickerbocker, The	NYC	New York-Boston-St. Louis	"	Electric; Steam
Kootenay Express	CP	Medicine Hat to Vancouver	"	Steam
L				
Lackawanna Limited	DL&W	Buffalo-New York	Standard	Diesel-Electric
Lake Cities, The	Erie	Chicago-Cleveland-Buffalo-New York	"	"
Lake Cities Special	NYC	Pittsburgh to Detroit	"	Steam
Lake Shore Limited	NYC	New York-Chicago	"	Electric; Steam
Land O'Corn	IC	Chicago-Waterloo, Iowa	Streamline	Diesel-Electric
Lark	SP	Los Angeles-San Francisco	"	Steam
LaSalle	CN;GTW	Montreal & Toronto to Detroit & Chicago	Standard	"
LaSalle Street Limited	CRI&P	Omaha to Chicago	"	"
Laurentian, The	NYC;D&H	New York-Montreal	"	Electric; Steam
Legion, The	PRR	New York to Washington	"	Electric
Legislator, The	PRR	New York-Washington	"	"
Liberty Limited	PRR	Washington-Chicago	Streamline	Electric; D-E
Lone Star	StLSW	Memphis-Shreveport-Dallas	Standard	Steam
Los Angeles Limited	C&NW;UP	Chicago-Los Angeles	"	Steam or D-E
Louisiana Limited	T&P	New Orleans-Shreveport-Dallas-Ft. Worth	"	Steam
Louisiane, The	IC	Chicago-Memphis-Jackson, Miss.-New Orleans (Hot Springs via CRI&P)	"	"
Louisville Daylight Express	PRR	Chicago to Louisville	"	"

Name of Train	Road(s) on which Operated	Between	Equipment	Power
M				
Mail	PRR	Pittsburgh-New York	Standard	Steam; Electric
Mail	NYC	New York-Buffalo & Cleveland to Chicago	"	Steam
Mail, The	GM&O	Chicago to St. Louis	"	Diesel-Electric
Manhattan Limited, The	PRR	New York-Washington-Chicago	"	Electric; Steam
Man-O'-War	CofGa.	Atlanta-Columbus	Streamline	Diesel-Electric
Maple Leaf, The	GTW;CN	Chicago-Toronto-Montreal	Standard	Steam
Maple Leaf, The	LV;Reading;CN	New York-Philadelphia-Buffalo-Toronto	"	Electric; Diesel-Electric; Steam
Maritime Express, The	CN	Montreal-Halifax	"	Steam
Mark Twain Zephyr	CB&Q	St. Louis-Burlington, Iowa	Streamline	Diesel-Electric
Marquette, The	CMStP&P	Chicago-Janesville-Madison-Mason City	Standard	
Marylander, The	B&O;Reading;CofNJ	Washington-New York	"	" "
Maumee, The	NYC	Chicago & Detroit to Cleveland	"	Steam
Mayflower, The	NYNH&H	New York-Boston	"	Diesel-Electric
Meadowlark	C&EI	Chicago-Cypress	Streamline	Steam
Memphian, The	StLSF	St. Louis-Memphis-Birmingham	Standard	
Memphis-Californian	CRI&P;SP	Memphis-Tucumcari-Los Angeles	"	"
Merchants Express	DL&W	Scranton to New York	"	"
Merchants Limited	NYNH&H	Boston-New York	"	D-E or Steam; Elect.
Mercury, The	NYC	Cleveland-Detroit-Chicago	Streamline	Steam
Meteor	StLSF	St. Louis-Oklahoma City	Standard	"
Metropolitan, The	PRR	New York to Pittsburgh	"	Steam; Electric
Metropolitan Special	B&O	St. Louis-Washington	"	Steam

Name of Train	Road(s) on which Operated	Between	Equipment	Power
Miamian	PRR;RF&P; ACL;FEC	New York-Washington-Miami	Standard	Electric; Steam; Diesel-Electric
Michigan, The	CP;NYC	Toronto to Detroit & Chicago	"	Steam
Michigan Special	NYC	Cincinnati to Toledo & Detroit	"	"
Mid-City Express	PRR;Wabash	Chicago-Detroit	"	"
Mid-Continent Special	CRI&P	Kansas City-St. Paul-Minneapolis	"	"
Midnight, The	Wabash	St. Louis-Chicago	"	"
Midnight Limited	Wabash	St. Louis-Kansas City	"	"
Midnight Special, The	GM&O	Chicago-St. Louis	"	Diesel-Electric
Midnight Special	NYC	Cleveland-Cincinnati	"	Steam
Midwest Hiawatha	CMStP&P	Chicago-Cedar Rapids-Marion-Des Moines-Omaha-Sioux City-Sioux Falls	Streamline	"
Mill Cities Limited	CGW	Minneapolis-Kansas City	Standard	"
Minnesota and Black Hills Express	C&NW	Chicago to Rapid City, S. D.	"	"
Minnesota "400"	C&NW	Chicago-Wyeville-Mankato	Streamline	"
Minnesota Marquette, The	CMStP&P	Chicago-Madison-Austin-Minneapolis	Standard	Steam; D-E
Minnesotan, The	CGW	Chicago-Minneapolis	"	Steam
Minute Man	B&M	Boston-Troy	"	Diesel-Electric
Miss Lou	IC	Jackson, Miss.,-New Orleans	Streamline	"
Missouri River Eagle	MP	St. Louis-Kansas City-St. Joseph-Lincoln-Omaha	"	" "
Missourian, The	MP	St. Louis-Kansas City	Standard	Steam
Missourian, The	NYC	St. Louis to Buffalo & New York	"	Steam; Electric
Mohawk, The (No. 5)	NYC	New York-Chicago	"	Electric; Steam

Name of Train	Road(s) on which Operated	Between	Equipment	Power
Mohawk Valley, The (No. 138)	NYC	Syracuse to Albany & New York	Standard	Steam; Electric
Monadnock	B&M	Boston to Bellows Falls	"	Steam
Mondamin, The	C&NW	Minneapolis-Sioux City-Omaha	"	"
Montreal Limited	NYC;D&H	New York-Montreal	"	Electric; Steam
Montrealer	PRR;NYNH&H; B&M;CV;CN	Washington-New York-Montreal	"	Electric; Diesel-Electric; Steam
Morning Daylight	SP	San Francisco-Los Angeles	Streamline	Steam
Morning Hiawatha	CMStP&P	Chicago-Milwaukee-St. Paul-Minneapolis	"	Diesel-Electric
Morning Puget Sounder	GN	Seattle-Vancouver	Standard	" "
Morning Star	StLSW	Memphis-Dallas	"	Steam
Morning Twin Cities Zephyrs	CB&Q	Chicago-St. Paul-Minneapolis	Streamline	Diesel-Electric
Motor City Special, The	NYC	Detroit-Chicago	Standard	Steam
Mt. Royal	NYC;B&M; Rutland;CN	New York-Boston-Montreal	"	Electric; Diesel-Electric; Steam
Mt. Vernon, The	PRR	New York-Washington	"	Electric
Mountain Express, The	Erie	New York to Binghamton, Elmira & Hornell	"	Steam
Mountain Special (s)	DL&W	Scranton-New York	"	"
Mountaineer (s)	B&M;MeC	Boston-Littleton-Bethlehem	"	Diesel-Electric
Mountaineer, The	D&RGW	Denver-Grand Junction-Montrose	"	Steam
Mountaineer, The (s)	NYO&W	New York to Roscoe	"	"
Mountaineer, The (s)	C&NW;Soo;CP	Chicago-St. Paul-Vancouver	"	"
Mountaineer-Indian Head Special (s)	C&NW	Chicago-Drummond	"	"
Murray Hill, The	NYNH&H	Boston to New York	"	D-E; Electric

Name of Train	Road(s) on which Operated	Between	Equipment	Power
Muskegon-Whitelake Week Ender (s)	C&O	Chicago-Muskegon	Standard	Steam
N				
Namekagon, The	C&NW	Minneapolis-Ashland	Standard	Steam
Nancy Hanks II	CofGa.	Atlanta-Savannah	Streamline	Diesel-Electric
Narragansett, The	NYNH&H	Boston-New York	Standard	Elect; D-E or Steam
Nathan Hale, The	NYNH&H	Springfield-New York	"	Steam; Electric
National Limited, The	B&O;Reading; CofNJ	St. Louis-Washington-New York	Streamline	Diesel-Electric
National Parks Special (s)	C&NW;UP	Chicago-Omaha-Denver	Standard	Steam
Naugatuck	NYNH&H	New York-Winsted	"	Electric; Steam
Nebraska Limited	CGW	Minneapolis to Omaha	"	Steam
Nebraska Zephyr	CB&Q	Chicago-Omaha-Lincoln	Streamline	Diesel-Electric
Neptune, The (s)	NYNH&H	New York-Woods Hole-Hyannis	Standard	Elect; D-E or Steam
New England States	NYC	Chicago-Boston	"	Steam
New England Wolverine	NYC	Boston to Detroit & Chicago	"	"
New Englander	B&M;CV;CN	Boston-Montreal	"	Diesel-Elect; Steam
New Englander, The	PRR	Pittsburgh to Philadelphia	"	Steam; Electric
New Englander, The—Quaker, The	PRR;NYNH&H	Pittsburgh to Philadelphia & Boston	"	" "
New York-Berkshire Exp.	NYC;NYNH&H	Boston & Springfield to Albany & New York	"	" "
New York-Boston Express	NYC;NYNH&H	New York to Boston	"	Electric; Steam
New York Express	NYC	Albany to New York	"	Steam; Electric
New York Express	LI	Montauk to New York	"	" "

Name of Train	Road(s) on which Operated	Between	Equipment	Power
New York Mail	DL&W	Buffalo to New York	Standard	Steam
New York Night Express	B&O;Reading; CofNJ	Washington to New York	"	Diesel-Electric
New York, Richmond and Norfolk Express	PRR;RF&P;N&W	New York to Richmond & Norfolk	"	Electric; Steam
New York Special (No. 44)	NYC	Chicago to Buffalo & New York	"	Steam; Electric
New York Special (No. 404)	NYC	Cincinnati to Buffalo & New York	"	" "
New Yorker, The	DL&W	Buffalo to New York	"	Steam
New Yorker, The	NYNH&H	Boston to New York	"	Diesel-Elect; Elect.
New Yorker, The	Southern;PRR	Atlanta-New York	"	" "
Newarker, The	CofNJ	Newark-Bay Head Junction	"	Steam
Niagara, The	NYC	New York & Boston to Buffalo-Niagara Falls	"	Electric; Steam
Niagara-Canadian, The	NYC	Chicago to Niagara Falls-Buffalo	"	Steam
Nickel Plate Limited	NYC&StL;DL&W	Chicago-Cleveland-Buffalo-New York	"	Diesel-Electric
Night Diamond, The	IC	Chicago-St. Louis	"	Steam
Night Express	C&O	Chicago-Grand Rapids-Muskegon	"	"
Night Express	CI&L	Chicago-Louisville	"	"
Night Hawk, The	CB&Q;GM&O	St. Louis-Kansas City	"	Diesel-Electric
Night White Mountains (s)	NYNH&H;B&M	New York-Bretton Woods	"	Elect; Steam or D-E
Nightingale, The	C&NW	Minneapolis-Omaha	"	Diesel-Electric
Noon Daylight	SP	San Francisco-Los Angeles	Streamline	Steam
Norfolk, Richmond and New York Express	N&W;RF&P;PRR	Norfolk to Richmond & New York	Standard	Steam; Electric
North American, The	C&NW	Minneapolis-Omaha	"	Diesel-Electric
North Coast Limited	CB&Q;NP;SP&S	Chicago-Minneapolis-Spokane-Seattle-Tacoma-Portland	Streamline	" "

Name of Train	Road(s) on which Operated	Between	Equipment	Power
North Shore Limited	NYC	New York-Chicago	Standard	Electric; Steam
North Star, The	NYC	New York to Lake Placid, Buffalo & Cleveland	"	"
North Western Limited	C&NW	Chicago-Minneapolis-Duluth	"	Diesel-Electric
North Wind (s)	NYNH&H;B&M	New York-Bretton Woods	"	Electric; D-E; Steam
North Woods Hiawatha	CMStP&P	Chicago-Minocqua	Streamline	Steam; D-E
Northeastern Limited	IC	Shreveport to Meridian	Standard	Steam
Northern Arrow, The (s)	PRR	St. Louis-Cincinnati-Chicago-Northern Michigan	"	"
Northern Express	PRR	Philadelphia & Washington to Erie	"	Electric; Steam
Northern Express	IC	New Orleans-Chicago	"	Steam
Northland, The	CN;T&NO	Toronto-North Bay-Timmins	"	"
Northwest Special	UP	Salt Lake City-Butte-Spokane	"	"
O				
Oakland Lark	SP	Los Angeles-Oakland	Streamline	"
Ocean Limited, The	CN	Halifax-Montreal	Standard	"
Ohio Special	NYC	Detroit & Toledo to Cincinnati	"	"
Ohio State Limited	NYC	New York-Cincinnati	"	Electric; Steam
Ohioan, The	PRR	Columbus-Chicago	"	Steam
Oil Flyer	Santa Fe	Kansas City-Tulsa	"	"
Oklahoman	StLSF	Kansas City-Tulsa	"	"
Old Dominion	RF&P	Richmond-Washington	Streamline	"
Olympian Hiawatha	CMStP&P	Chicago-Milwaukee-Seattle-Tacoma	"	Diesel-Electric
Omaha Express	CGW	Minneapolis to Omaha	Standard	Steam
Omaha Limited	Wabash	St. Louis to Omaha	"	"
On Wisconsin	CMStP&P	Milwaukee-Madison	"	"

Name of Train	Road(s) on which Operated	Between	Equipment	Power
Onondaga, The	NYC	Cleveland & Buffalo to New York	Standard	Steam; Electric
Ontarian, The	NYC;TH&B;CP	New York-Toronto	"	Electric; Steam
Ontario Limited, The	CN	Detroit-Toronto	"	Steam
Orange Blossom Special (w)	PRR;RF&P;SAL	New York-Washington-Miami-Tampa-St. Petersburg	"	Electric; Steam; Diesel-Electric
Oriental Limited	CB&Q;GN;SP&S	Chicago-Seattle-Portland	"	D-E; Steam; Electric
Orleanean, The	MP	New Orleans-Houston	"	Steam
Overland, San Francisco	C&NW;UP;SP	(See San Francisco Overland)		
Overnighter	NYNH&H;B&M	New York-Woodsville-Berlin, N.H.	"	Electric; Steam
Overseas, The	CP	Detroit-Montreal	"	Steam
Owl (Nos. 57-58)	SP	San Francisco-Los Angeles	"	"
Owl, The	CN	Regina-Saskatoon-Prince Albert	"	"
Owl, The	DL&W	New York-Scranton-Binghamton-Syracuse-Buffalo	"	"
Owl, The	NYNH&H	Boston-New York	"	Electric; D-E
Owl, The (Nos. 17-18)	SP	Houston-Ft. Worth-Dallas	"	Steam
Ozarker, The	MP	St. Louis-Little Rock	"	"
P				
Pacemaker, The	NYC	New York-Chicago	Streamline	Electric; Steam
Pacific-Pony Express	C&NW;UP	Chicago-Kansas City-Los Angeles-Portland	Standard	Steam or D-E
Pacific Express	Erie	New York to Chicago	"	Diesel-Electric
Palmetto	PRR;RF&P;ACL	New York-Washington-Wilmington-Augusta-Charleston-Savannah	"	Electric; Steam; Diesel-Electric
Palmland, The	PRR;RF&P;SAL	New York-Washington-Miami-Tampa-St. Petersburg	"	" "

Top-left

Name of Train	Road(s) on which Operated	Between	Equipment	Power
Pan-American, The	L&N	Cincinnati-New Orleans	Standard	Diesel-Electric
Panama Limited	IC	Chicago-St. Louis-New Orleans	Streamline	"
Partridge, The	LI	New York-Port Jefferson	Standard	Electric; Steam
Passenger, Mail and Exp.	RF&P;SAL	Washington-Jacksonville	"	Steam
Patriot, The	B&M	Bedford-Boston	"	"
Patriot, The	NYNH&H;PRR	Boston-New York-Washington	"	D-E; Electric
Paul Revere, The	B&M	Boston-Bedford	"	Steam
Paul Revere, The	NYC	Chicago-Boston	"	"
Peach Queen, The	PRR;Southern	New York-Washington-Atlanta	"	Electric; D-E
Peconic Bay Express	LI	New York-Greenport	"	Electric; Steam
Pelican, The	PRR;Southern; N&W;Southern	New York-Williamson-Birmingham-Shreveport-New Orleans	"	Electric; Steam; Diesel-Electric
Peninsula "400"	C&NW	Chicago-Fond du Lac-Menominee-Ishpeming	Streamline	Diesel-Electric
Pennsylvania Limited	PRR	New York-Chicago	Standard	Electric; Steam
Pennsylvanian, The	PRR	New York-Chicago	"	Electric; D-E
Penobscot	B&M;MeC	Boston-Bangor	"	Steam
*Peoria-Chicago Rocket	CRI&P	Peoria to Chicago	Streamline	Diesel-Electric
**Pere Marquettes	C&O	Detroit-Grand Rapids	"	"
Pershing Square, The	NYNH&H	Boston to New York	Standard	"
Philadelphia Express	B&O	Washington to Philadelphia	"	Steam
Philadelphia Express	PRR	Pittsburgh to Philadelphia	"	Steam; Electric
Philadelphia Flyer	CofPa;Reading	Scranton to Philadelphia	"	"
Philadelphia Night Express	PRR	Pittsburgh to Philadelphiz	"	Steam; Electric
Philadelphia-Washington Express	PRR	Philadelphia to Washington	"	Electric

*Two trips daily.
**Three trips daily.

Top-right

Name of Train	Road(s) on which Operated	Between	Equipment	Power
Piedmont Limited	PRR;Southern; A&WP;WofAla; L&N	New York-Washington-Atlanta-New Orleans	Standard	Electric; Diesel-Electric or Steam
Pilgrim, The	PRR;NYNH&H	Philadelphia-Boston	"	Elect; Steam or D-E
Pine Tree	B&M;MeC	Boston-Portland-Bangor	"	Diesel-Electric
Pioneer, The	MP	Houston-Corpus Christi-Brownsville	"	Steam
Pioneer Limited, The	CMStP&P	Chicago-St. Paul-Minneapolis	"	Diesel-Electric
Pioneer Zephyr	CB&Q	Lincoln-McCook	Streamline	"
Pittsburgh-Buffalo Express (No. 284)	NYC	Pittsburgh to Buffalo & Boston	Standard	Steam
Pittsburgh-Buffalo Express (No. 272)	NYC	Pittsburgh to Buffalo & Toronto	"	"
Pittsburgh-Cleveland Exp.	DL&W	Buffalo to Cleveland & Pittsburgh	"	"
Pittsburgh Express	DL&W	Scranton to Pittsburgh	"	"
Pittsburgh Night Express	PRR	Philadelphia to Pittsburgh	"	Electric; Steam
Pittsburgh "79"	B&O	Washington to Pittsburgh	"	Steam
Pittsburgh Special	NYC	Chicago & Detroit to Pittsburgh	"	"
Pittsburgher, The	PRR	New York-Pittsburgh	Streamline	Electric; Steam
Planter, The	IC	Memphis-New Orleans	Standard	Steam
Pocahontas, The	N&W	Cincinnati-Columbus-Norfolk	"	"
Pocono Express	DL&W	Buffalo to New York	"	"
Ponce de Leon	NYC;Southern; SAL	Chicago-Detroit-Cleveland-Jacksonville-St. Petersburg	"	Steam; Diesel-Electric
Pony Express	UP	Kansas City to Los Angeles	"	Steam or D-E
Portland Rose	C&NW;UP	Chicago-Portland	"	Steam
Portsmouth Down	B&M	Portsmouth to Boston	"	"

Middle-left

Name of Train	Road(s) on which Operated	Between	Equipment	Power
Portsmouth Up	B&M	Boston to Portsmouth	Standard	Steam
Potatoland Special	BAR	Bangor-Van Buren	"	"
Potomac, The	PRR	New York-Washington	"	Electric
Powhatan Arrow, The	N&W	Norfolk-Cincinnati	Streamline	Steam
Prairie State, The	NYC	Cleveland to Chicago	Standard	"
Prairie State Express, The	GM&O	St. Louis to Chicago	"	Diesel-Electric
President, The	PRR	New York-Washington	"	Electric
Prospector	D&RGW	Denver-Salt Lake City	"	Diesel-Electric
Puget Sounder	GN	(See Afternoon Puget Sounder and Morning Puget Sounder)		
Puritan, The	NYNH&H	Boston-New York	"	D-E; Electric

Q

Quaker, The	NYNH&H;PRR	Boston-Philadelphia	Standard	D-E or Steam; Elect.
Queen and Crescent	Southern	Cincinnati-Chattanooga-Birmingham-New Orleans	"	D-E; Steam
Queen of the Valley	Reading;CofPa; CofNJ	Harrisburg-New York	"	Steam

R

Rainbow, The	PRR	Chicago-New York	Standard	Steam; Electric
Rainbow Special, The	MP	Kansas City-Little Rock-Hot Springs	"	Steam
Ranger, The	Santa Fe	Galveston-Houston-Ft. Worth-Dallas-Kansas City-Chicago	"	"
Rapidio de Laredo	NdeM	Neuvo Laredo-Mexico City	"	"
(See Sunshine Special)				

Middle-right

Name of Train	Road(s) on which Operated	Between	Equipment	Power
Rebel, The (See also Gulf Coast Rebel)	GM&O	St. Louis-Jackson, Tenn.-Jackson, Miss.-New Orleans	Streamline	Diesel-Electric
Red Arrow, The	PRR	New York-Washington-Detroit	Standard	Electric; D-E
Red Bird, The	PRR;Wabash	Chicago-Detroit	"	Steam
Red River Limited	GN	Minneapolis-St. Paul-Grand Forks	"	Diesel-Electric
Red Wing	B&M;CP	Boston-Montreal	"	D-E; Steam
Representative, The	PRR	New York-Washington	"	Electric
Resort Special (s)	C&O	Chicago-Detroit-Grand Rapids-Petoskey-Bay View	"	Steam
Rochester-Minnesota Spl.	C&NW	Chicago-Rochester-Rapid City	"	"
Rocky Mountain Rocket	CRI&P	Chicago-Denver-Colorado Springs	Streamline	Diesel-Electric
Roger Williams, The	NYNH&H	New York-Boston	Standard	Electric; Steam
Rogue River	SP	Portland-Ashland	"	Steam
Royal Blue, The	B&O;Reading; CofNJ	Washington-Baltimore-Philadelphia-New York	Streamline	Diesel-Electric
Royal Gorge	MP;D&RGW;WP	St. Louis-Pueblo-San Francisco	Standard	Steam
Royal Palm	NYC;Southern	Chicago-Detroit-Cleveland-Jacksonville	"	Steam;D-E
Royal Poinciana (w)	FEC	Jacksonville-Miami	"	Steam
Royal York	CP	Montreal-Toronto-Detroit	"	"

S

Sacramento Daylight	SP	Sacramento-Los Angeles	Streamline	Steam
St. Louis Limited	Wabash	Omaha-St. Louis	Standard	"
St. Louis Limited	Wabash	Des Moines-St. Louis	"	"
St. Louis Limited	Wabash	Detroit-St. Louis	"	"
St. Louis Special	NYC	Cleveland & Cincinnati to St. Louis	"	"

Bottom-left

Name of Train	Road(s) on which Operated	Between	Equipment	Power
St. Louis Special	Wabash	Detroit-St. Louis	Standard	Diesel-Electric
St. Louisan, The	PRR	New York-Washington-St. Louis	"	Electric; D-E
Sam Houston Zephyr	FW&DC;BRI	Ft. Worth-Dallas-Houston	Streamline	Diesel-Electric
*San Diegan	Santa Fe	Los Angeles-San Diego	"	"
San Francisco Overland	C&NW;UP;SP	Chicago-San Francisco	Standard	Steam
San Joaquin Daylight	SP	San Francisco-Los Angeles	Streamline	"
**San Juan	D&RGW	Alamosa-Durango	Standard	"
Scotian, The	CN	Montreal-Halifax	"	"
Scout, The	Santa Fe	Chicago-Los Angeles-Oakland	"	"
Scranton Flyer	Reading;CofPa.	Philadelphia-Scranton	"	"
Scrantonian	DL&W	New York to Scranton	"	Electric; D-E or Steam
Seashore Express, The (s)	NYNH&H	New York-Providence	"	Steam
Seminole	IC;CofGa;ACL; FEC	Chicago-St. Louis-Savannah-Tampa-St. Petersburg	"	Steam
Senator, The	NYNH&H;PRR	Boston-New York-Washington	"	D-E; Electric
Senator, The	SP	San Francisco-Sacramento	"	Steam
Seneca, The	NYC	New York-Rochester	"	Electric; Steam
Shasta, The	SP	San Francisco-Grant's Pass	"	Steam
Shasta Daylight	SP	(Announced to be installed in 1948)	"	
Shenandoah, The	B&O;Reading; CofNJ	Chicago-Washington-New York	"	Diesel-Electric
Shinnecock Express	LI	New York to Montauk	"	Electric; Steam
Shoreland "400"	C&NW	Chicago-Manitowoc-Green Bay	Streamline	Diesel-Electric
Shoreliner, The	NYNH&H	New York-Boston	Standard	Electric; D-E
Short Line Express	CRI&P	Minneapolis-Kansas City	"	Steam

*Four round trips daily.
**Narrow gauge.

Bottom-right

Name of Train	Road(s) on which Operated	Between	Equipment	Power
Short Line Flyer	FW&DC;BRI	Dallas-Houston	Standard	Gas-Electric
Shreveporter, The	L&A;KCS	Shreveport-Hope	"	Diesel-Electric
Sierra	SP	San Francisco-Sacramento	"	Steam
Silver Comet, The	PRR;RF&P;SAL	New York-Washington-Richmond-Birmingham	Streamline	Electric; Steam; Diesel-Electric
Silver Meteor, The	PRR;RF&P;SAL	New York-Washington-Miami-St. Petersburg-Sarasota-Venice	"	" " "
Silver Star, The (w)	PRR;RF&P;SAL	New York-Washington-Richmond-Miami-Tampa-St. Petersburg	"	" " "
Silver Streak Zephyr	CB&Q	Kansas City-Omaha-Lincoln	"	"
Sinnissippi, The	IC	Chicago-Freeport	Standard	Steam
Sioux, The	CMStP&P	Chicago-Milwaukee-Mason City-Mitchell-Rapid City	"	"
Ski Meister, The (w)	NYNH&H	New York-Waterbury, Vt.	"	Electric; D-E;Steam
Skier (w)	B&M	Boston-North Conway-Intervale	"	Diesel-Electric
Skyland Special	Southern	Asheville-Charlotte-Jacksonville	"	Steam
Soo-Dominion	C&NW;Soo;CP	Chicago-St. Paul-Vancouver	"	"
Sooner, The	MKT	Kansas City-Oklahoma City	"	"
South Shore Express	NYC	New York & Boston to Buffalo & Chicago	"	Electric; Steam
South Shore Express	LI	New York-Montauk	"	"
Southern Belle	KCS;L&A	Kansas City-New Orleans	Streamline	Diesel-Electric
Southern Express	PRR	Erie to Washington & Philadelphia	Standard	Steam; Electric
Southern Express	IC	Chicago to New Orleans	"	Steam
Southern Scenic	MP	Memphis-Kansas City	"	"
Southern Tier Express	Erie	Buffalo & Hornell to New York	"	"
Southerner, The	PRR;Southern	New York-Washington-New Orleans	Streamline	Electric; D-E

Name of Train	Road(s) on which Operated	Between	Equipment	Power
Southerner, The	MP;T&P	St. Louis-Memphis-Dallas-El Paso-Houston-San Antonio-Laredo	Standard	Steam
Southland, The (East Coast)	PRR;L&N;CofGa; ACL;FEC	Chicago-Cincinnati-Atlanta-Albany-Jacksonville-Miami	"	Steam; D-E
Southland, The (West Coast)	PRR;Wabash;L&N; CofGa;ACL	Chicago-Detroit-Cincinnati-Atlanta Albany-Tampa-St. Petersburg	"	" "
Southwest Express	CRI&P;SP	Chicago-Tucumcari-Los Angeles	"	Steam
Southwest Limited, The	CMStP&P	Chicago also Milwaukee-Excelsior Springs-Kansas City	"	Diesel-Electric
Southwestern Limited	IC	Meridian to Shreveport	"	Steam
Southwestern Limited	NYC	St. Louis-New York-Boston	"	D-E; Electric
South Wind, The	PRR;L&N;ACL; FEC	Chicago-Miami	Streamline	Steam; Diesel-Electric
Speaker, The	PRR	New York-Washington	Standard	Electric
"Spirit of St. Louis"	PRR	New York-Washington-St. Louis	Streamline	Electric; D-E
Spokane, The	UP	Spokane-Portland	Standard	Steam
Sportsman, The	C&O	Washington-Norfolk-Cincinnati-Louisville-Detroit	"	"
Star, The	LV	New York-Philadelphia-Buffalo	"	Electric; D-E
State of Maine	NYNH&H;B&M	New York-Portland	"	"
Streamliner "400"	C&NW	Menominee-Chicago	Streamline	Diesel-Electric
Sunbeam	SP	Houston-Dallas	"	Steam
Sunchaser, The (w)	IC;CofGa;ACL; FEC	Chicago & St. Louis-Birmingham-Albany-Jacksonville-Miami	Standard	"
Sundown, The	NYNH&H	Boston-New York	"	D-E or Steam; Elect.
Sunflower, The	MP	St. Louis-Wichita	"	Steam

Name of Train	Road(s) on which Operated	Between	Equipment	Power
Sunnyland, The	StLSF;Southern	St. Louis-Memphis-Birmingham-Atlanta	Standard	Steam
Sunset Limited	SP	Los Angeles-New Orleans	"	"
Sunshine Special, The (First Section)	PRR;MP;T&P; NdeM	New York-Washington-St.Louis-Dallas-Ft. Worth-El Paso-Houston-Galveston-San Antonio-Mexico City	"	Electric; Steam; Diesel-Electric
Sunshine Special, The (Second Section)	NYC;C&O;MP; T&P;SP;NdeM	New York-Washington-St. Louis-Memphis-Dallas-Fort Worth-El Paso-Los Angeles-Houston-Galveston-San Antonio-Mexico City	"	" "
Sunshine Special, The (Third Section)	MP;T&P;KCS	St. Louis-Memphis-El Dorado-Houston-Galveston-Brownsville-Shreveport-Lake Charles-New Orleans	"	Diesel-Electric
Super Chief, The	Santa Fe	Chicago-Los Angeles	Streamline	" "
Susquehannock, The	PRR	Philadelphia-Williamsport	Standard	Electric; Steam
Sycamore, The	NYC	Cincinnati & Indianapolis to Chicago	"	Steam

T

Tennessean, The	PRR;Southern; N&W;Southern	New York-Washington-Lynchburg-Bristol-Knoxville-Chattanooga-Nashville-Memphis	Streamline	Electric; Diesel-Electric; Steam
Texan, The	MP;T&P	St. Louis-Memphis-Dallas-Ft. Worth-Houston	Standard	Steam
Texas-Colorado Limited	T&P	Ft. Worth-New Orleans	"	"

Name of Train	Road(s) on which Operated	Between	Equipment	Power
Texas Eagle	MP	(Announced to be installed in 1948)		
Texas Limited	IC	Meridian to Shreveport	Standard	Steam
Texas Rocket	CRI&P	Ft. Worth-Dallas-Oklahoma City-Kansas City	Streamline	Diesel-Electric
Texas Special	StLSF;MKT	St. Louis-Dallas-Ft. Worth-San Antonio-Houston	Standard	Steam or Diesel-Electric
Texas Triangle	MP	Ft. Worth-Houston-San Antonio-Corpus Christi-Laredo	"	Steam
Texas Zephyr	C&S;FW&DC	Denver-Ft. Worth-Dallas	Streamline	Diesel-Electric
Thoroughbred, The	CI&L	Louisville-Chicago	"	" "
Tippecanoe	CI&L	Chicago-Indianapolis	Standard	Steam
Toledo-Detroit Express	NYC	Indianapolis to Toledo & Detroit	"	"
Tomahawk, The	CMStP&P	Chicago-Wausau-Minocqua-Woodruff	"	Steam; D-E
Toronto-Buffalo Express	NYC	Toronto-Buffalo-New York	"	Steam; Electric
Trail Blazer, The	PRR	New York-Chicago	Streamline	Electric; D-E
Traveler, The	CMStP&P	Milwaukee to Chicago	Standard	Steam
Tulsan, The	Santa Fe	Chicago-Kansas City-Tulsa	Streamline	Diesel-Electric
Tuscarora, The	NYC	New York-Rochester-Buffalo	Standard	Electric; Steam
Tuxedo, The	Erie	New York-Port Jervis	"	Steam
Twentieth Century Limited	NYC	Chicago-New York	Streamline	Electric; D-E
Twilight Limited, The	NYC	Chicago-Detroit	Standard	Steam
Twin Cities "400"	C&NW	Chicago-St. Paul-Minneapolis	Streamline	Diesel-Electric
Twin City Express	CGW	Omaha to Minneapolis	Standard	Steam
Twin City Limited	CGW	Omaha to Minneapolis	"	"
Twin Star Rocket	CRI&P;BRI	Minneapolis-Kansas City-Ft. Worth-Dallas-Houston	Streamline	Diesel-Electric

Name of Train	Road(s) on which Operated	Between	Equipment	Power
Twin Zephyrs	CB&Q	(See Morning Zephyrs and Afternoon Zephyrs)		

U

Union, The	PRR	Chicago-Cincinnati	Standard	Steam
Upstate Special	NYC	New York to Utica	"	Electric; Steam
Utahn	UP	Portland-Boise-Pocatello-Salt Lake City	"	Steam or D-E

V

Vacationer (w)	PRR;RF&P; ACL;FEC	New York-Miami	Standard	Electric; Steam; Diesel-Electric
Valley Express	NYC	Chicago to Saginaw & Bay City	"	Steam
Valley Special	PRR	Chicago to Pittsburgh	"	"
Valley "400"	C&NW	Green Bay-Fond du Lac-Chicago	Streamline	Diesel-Electric
Varsity, The	CMStP&P	Chicago-Janesville-Madison	Standard	" "
Vermonter, The	CV;B&M; NYNH&H	St. Albans-White River Junction-New York	"	Steam; Electric
Victory, The	C&NW	Chicago-Minneapolis	"	Steam; D-E
Victory-Fast Mail, The	C&NW	Chicago-Duluth	"	Steam
Viger, The	CP	Montreal-Quebec	"	"
Viking, The	C&NW	Chicago-Minneapolis	"	"

W

*Wall Street	Reading;CofNJ	Philadelphia-New York	Streamline	Steam

*To begin operating early in 1948.

Name of Train	Road(s) on which Operated	Between	Equipment	Power
Washington and Philadelphia Express	PRR	Buffalo to Philadelphia & Washington	Standard	Steam; Electric
Washington "80"	B&O	Pittsburgh to Washington	"	Steam
Washington Express	B&O	Philadelphia to Washington	"	"
Washington Night Express	CofNJ;Reading; B&O	New York to Baltimore & Washington	"	Diesel-Electric
Washington-Pittsburgh-Chicago Express	B&O	Washington to Chicago	"	" "
Washingtonian	CN;CV;B&M; NYNH&H;PRR	Montreal to New York & Washington	"	Steam; Diesel-Electric; Electric
Washingtonian, The	B&O;P&LE;Erie	Baltimore-Washington-Pittsburgh-Cleveland	"	Steam
Water Level, The	NYC	Chicago-New York	"	Steam; Electric
West Coast	SP	Los Angeles-Portland-Dunsmuir-Los Angeles	"	Steam
West Virginia Night Express	B&O	Chicago-Wheeling	"	"
West Virginian, The	B&O	Washington-Parkersburg	"	"
Westerner, The	DL&W;NYC&StL	New York to Chicago	"	Diesel-Electric
Whippoorwill, The	C&EI	Chicago-Evansville	Streamline	" "
White City Special	NYC	Cincinnati-Indianapolis-Chicago	Standard	Steam
Will Rogers, The	StLSF	St. Louis to Oklahoma City	"	"
William Penn, The	PRR;NYNH&H	Philadelphia-Boston	"	Electric; D-E
Winnipeg Limited, The	GN	St. Paul-Winnipeg	"	Diesel-Electric
Winnipeger, The	CP;Soo	Winnipeg-St. Paul-Minneapolis	"	Steam
Winnipesaukee (s)	B&M	Boston-Plymouth, N. H.	"	Diesel-Electric
Wolverine, The	NYC	New York-Boston-Chicago	"	Electric; Steam

Name of Train	Road(s) on which Operated	Between	Equipment	Power
Y				
Yankee Clipper, The	NYNH&H	Boston-New York	Standard	D-E; Electric
Yellowstone Special (s)	UP	Salt Lake City-West Yellowstone	"	Steam
Z				
Zephyr Rocket	CB&Q;CRI&P	St. Louis-St. Paul-Minneapolis	Streamline	Diesel-Electric

Two colorful passenger trains—a Chicago & North-Western commuter and a Milwaukee Road through passenger—pause at Milwaukee's main passenger station. In the 1948 Official Guide of the Railways, *the Milwaukee Road boasted it had the only road operating over its own rails all the way between Chicago and the Pacific Northwest. The Milwaukee's* Pioneer Limited *in 1948 ran between Chicago and Milwaukee in only 1 hour and 40 minutes, while the* Morning Hiawatha *was even quicker with an elasped time of 1 hour and 22 minutes. Chris Burritt*

A six-wheel heavyweight observation car tacked on the rear of a passenger train at Milwaukee's Union Station was reason for a bystander to be curious. Where was the car going? Who was riding in it? Were the occupants of the car traveling for business or pleasure? Chris Burritt

FOR ALL-OUT TRAVEL PLEASURE, RIDE ON CARS
BUILT BY PULLMAN-STANDARD

Go by TRAIN!

the eye-level way...

Railways are scenic *eye-level* ways—comfortable, dependable, safe; unhampered by weather or traffic congestion—the most popular of all travel ways.

To bring you everything that makes a trip worthwhile, the great railways of America are adding whole fleets of the very finest in new cars from the shops of Pullman-Standard.

You'll find salon smartness when you go by train, and sleeping comfort to match... privacy, or social get-together... night club gayety, or an easy chair with a book... meals to your taste... loads of room

to move about from one fascinating car to another... while the passing parade of America flashes by at eye level.

PULLMAN-STANDARD has led in creating the cars of today... FIRST in presenting new car designs... FIRST to build and deliver these cars... FIRST in volume production. Pullman-Standard is Sleeping Car Headquarters and the leader in all types of railway car building.

Assure yourself of the safest and finest accommodations on the world's best railroads. Look for the Pullman-Standard nameplate on each car.

PULLMAN-STANDARD *Car Manufacturing Company*

CHICAGO · ILLINOIS   Offices in six cities from coast to coast... Manufacturing plants at six strategic points

World's largest builders of modern streamlined railroad cars

© 1946, P-S. Ci M. CO.

The Pullman-Standard Car Manufacturing Company promoted rail travel throughout America, which in the end helped the company to sell more railroad cars. "...Salon smartness, privacy, easy chair with a book, meals to your taste, loads of room to move about..." were some of the advertised features of using the rails for transportation.

41

In 1947 the Maine Central and Boston & Maine re-equipped three premier coach trains between Boston, Portland and Bangor. On this new 2,000-hp EMD-produced E-7, the distinctive pine tree logo is emblazoned on the nose. EMD

WAY DOWN EAST: B&M/MEC REVISITED

In 1947 the carbuilder log jam eased, and expanded services with new trains suddenly exploded. From coast to coast, hardly a month went by without some new service being introduced with maximum flair and public relations skill. Tomorrow could not be brighter, even in staid northern New England.

In 1945 the jointly-operated Boston & Maine/Maine Central railroads placed an order for four baggage-coaches, four restaurant-lounges, and 16 coach-smokers from Pullman-Standard and 20 E-7's from Electro-Motive. Delivery was piece-meal, but by fall, 1947 enough of the cars had arrived to allow the re-equipping of the B&M/MeC's three premier coach trains in Boston-Portland-Bangor service. New matching diesels hauled the newly streamlined *Kennebec*, *Flying Yankee* and *Pine Tree*.

The baggage-coaches seated 36 with another eight in a partitioned smoking lounge. The full coaches seated 56—with 10 more passengers in a fully glass-enclosed, separately vented smoking lounge. Each restaurant-lounge car seated 24 for meals and 18 in the lounge area.

Six of the coaches had a predominantly yellow interior, another six had green and the final four were blue—matching the coach section in the baggage-coaches. Window drapes in all cars were cedar color inside with an aluminized exterior finish. The restaurant-lounge cars had oval mirrors on the restaurant end bulkheads and curved photomurals on the lounge end. Overstuffed upholstered chairs filled the lounge while bench seats for four patrons filled alcoves and parties of two were seated at triangular tables in the dining section. The alcoves were separated from the remainder of the car with low partitions. The curved glass partition tops contained either a B&M Minuteman or MeC Pine Tree logo etched into the surface.

The public received the new equipment enthusiastically. Their interest had been especially raised with a multi-state contest for elementary school children to name the various cars. Winners unveiled the nameboard of specific cars in a public ceremony. Their school and town were included on the nameboard, and the child and their schoolmates were featured guests at the ceremony. Names such as *Arundel, Merrymeeting, Snow Bird* and *Hermit Thrush* adorned the cars, and have joined the collective memory of Northern New England.

The opening of the parallel Maine turnpike in 1947 was but an insignificant speck on the horizon.

THE NEW HAVEN: SCROD, SOCIETY AND STREAMLINERS

With nearly 50% of its gross revenues derived from passenger service, the New York, New Haven & Hartford Railroad was—to put it mildly—pro passenger. In 1935-39 it had pioneered the semi-streamlined lightweight passenger coach in a joint effort with industrial designer Walter Teague and Pullman-Standard's Worcester, Massachusetts, Osgood Bradley works. Designed in a tubular fashion to omit the traditional center sill, the car saved 15 tons and eventually the New Haven fleet totalled 205 cars.

Several other roads ordered the basic design including Boston & Maine, Lehigh Valley, Kansas City Southern and others. A total of more than 300 cars including coaches, grill, baggage, combination and baggage-mail configurations were constructed before WWII.

The car was so popular on the New Haven that A. C. Gilbert, New Haven-based manufacturer of American Flyer trains, copied them in his new toy train line. Accurate or not with old New Haven employees, the cars will forevermore be remembered as "American Flyer" cars. Perhaps it is the ultimate tribute to Teague, the New Haven and Pullman.

Building upon its past success, the NH had all but the sleeper portion of its postwar passenger fleet predicated upon that prewar American Flyer design, the only road so to do. An order for 180

A Bronx, Martini or Manhattan from this 1948 New Haven grill car menu would set you back just $.60. A tuna salad sandwich was $.50, and roast leg of lamb with brown gray, candied sweet potatoes, fresh spinach and a roll, only $1.25.

ATLANTIC COAST LINE   FLORIDA EAST COAST

A New Era with General Motors Diesels

200 Passenger Units Now Operate over 30,000,000 Miles Per Year
Finer Trains—Larger Power Units—Bring Greater Revenues

A General Motors ad tells the story: more speed and better maintenance provided by diesels helped transform the nation's motive power. In a 1946 performance test over a 15 day period using a number of diesels and steam engines, diesels required 288 hours of shop work, while steam locomotives needed 672 hours. Diesels were less affected by the cold, had lower centers of gravity, reduced track stresses, provided cleaner operation and had higher availability than steam locomotives.

THE year 1934 heralded the beginning of a new era in rail transportation. The marked advances which have occurred during these seven short years constitute one of the crowning achievements in all railroad history. While a number of factors are responsible for this change from former standards, one thing stands out — the application of the GM Diesel engine to main line passenger operation.

From the humble beginning of the Burlington's "Pioneer Zephyr," the first high-speed Diesel-powered passenger train in the United States, the use of GM Diesels has expanded without interruption until to-day (October 1941) 200 GM Diesel passenger units are operating more than 30,000,000 miles per year in revenue service on 21 Class 1 railroads.

The universal public acceptance of this new clean, smooth, comfortable, fast, safe transportation soon resulted in larger trains and more of them. The "Pioneer Zephyr" comprised three articulated cars including the power car, the forward portion of which housed the General Motors 600-hp. Diesel engine. Compare this with the latest "City of Los

Angeles," a 17-car train powered by a 6000-hp. GM Diesel, which makes the 2,299 miles from Chicago to Los Angeles in 39¾ hours — an average speed of 58 m. p. h. Other outstanding high-speed long distance trains are the Santa Fe "Super Chief," the Burlington "Denver Zephyrs" and the Baltimore and Ohio "Capitol Limited," with average speeds up to 66 m. p. h.

Contrary to the old belief that passenger traffic was a "necessary evil" and that freight business had to carry the entire load, GM Diesels in passenger service have proved to be profitable investments. One of the most outstanding examples of how GM Diesels make passenger service pay is shown in the figures from the Rock Island's comparative study of two GM Diesel-powered "Rocky Mountain Rockets" (12 months' operation ending June 30, 1941) and two steam trains (12 months' operation ending October 31, 1939) operating in the same service between Chicago-Denver and Colorado Springs. The two GM Diesel-powered trains showed a profit of $513,559.00 while the two steam trains showed a loss of $28,637.00 — a difference of $542,196.00.

ARD   SOUTHERN   BALTIMORE & OHIO

High Availability Distinguishes GM Diesel Performance
Record of 97 Per Cent Consistently Maintained with Heavy Trains on Long Runs

ALTHOUGH the national record for availability stands at 97 per cent, the performance of GM Diesels on individual railroads has exceeded even this figure.

On the Chicago-Twin Cities run of the Chicago and North Western, two 4,000-hp. GM Diesel locomotives, each making two round trips of 800 miles daily, have operated more than 1,200,000 miles with an availability record of 100 per cent. Five steam locomotives were formerly required for this service.

On the Baltimore & Ohio, one of the GM passenger Diesels operated more than a year between Chicago and Washington, D. C., without missing a trip. Further records from the Baltimore & Ohio show that nine GM Diesels operated 4,413,894 miles with an availability of 95.4 per cent.

On the Burlington, the 3,000-hp."Denver Zephyrs" which have been making one of the fastest long runs in the world since 1936, operated nearly 1,500,000 miles at an average schedule speed of 66.4 miles per hour before they were taken out for general

overhaul. On this particular run, two steam locomotives for each train would be required even to approach the Diesel record. GM Diesel operation on the Burlington shows over 15,000,000 miles with an availability record of 97 per cent.

On the Rock Island, 13 GM Diesels recorded a figure of 98.2 per cent availability in operating 5,459,655 miles.

Performance figures such as these certainly indicate in no uncertain terms that the old order of locomotive performance must give way to this new order of the day.

CONFIDENCE

Confidence in a product and in those who make it results only from long satisfactory dealings and proved superiority of performance and service. Fundamental, of course, is the element of quality. It is highly significant that 99 per cent of the Diesel high-speed passenger trains in this country are powered with General Motors Locomotives.

GENERAL MOTORS LOCOMOTIVES

45

Above: BURLINGTON—4000-Hp. Diesel Passenger Locomotive

Above: SANTA FE—4000-Hp. Diesel Passenger Locomotive

Above: MISSOURI PACIFIC—2000-Hp. Diesel Passenger Locomotive   Below: ROCK ISLAND—2000-Hp. Diesel Passenger Locomotive

The paint schemes of passenger diesels, being the most visual aspect of these machines, gives the traveling public an impression of the level of service one could expect on board. The Santa Fe achieved a high degree of success with their passenger paint schemes, and attained a superb level of service.

Above: THE MILWAUKEE ROAD—4000-Hp. Diesel Passenger Locomotive

Above: ILLINOIS CENTRAL—4000-Hp. Diesel Passenger Locomotive

Above: KANSAS CITY SOUTHERN—2000-Hp. Diesel Passenger Locomotive. Below: BOSTON AND MAINE—600-Hp. Diesel-Powered Unit

The Milwaukee Road's
Olympian Hiawatha *entered service June 29, 1947, cutting 14 hours from the previous transcontinental service. The* Illinois Central *placed the* City of New Orleans *in service in April of 1947 and by its 94th day, the train had grossed $1 million, with expected annual gross of $6.2 million. These dramatic railroad successes were common in the postwar era where technology and streamlining were starting to pay off.*

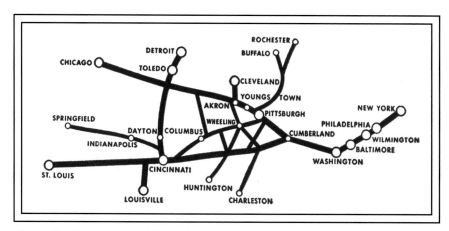

Generalized route map of the Baltimore & Ohio RR

baggage-lounges, coaches, diners, parlors and two tavern-observations was placed with Pullman in 1947. Immediate delivery, please, from the Pullman-Bradley plant in Worcester. The only major change to the prewar design was the use of stainless steel sheathing clipped to the Cor-Ten steel sides.

Later, an additional order for 27 sleepers of standard Pullman streamliner construction was added to the overall order. Only they, plus the 10 diners and two tavern-observations, were completed in Pullman's Chicago works.

Slowly, the massive NH order wound its way through Pullman's Osgood Bradley plant in Worcester. By late 1947 cars begin arriving and continued to do so through 1949. Concurrently, twenty-seven 2,000-hp PA passenger locomotives arrived from Alco/GE to pull the new equipment. Locomotives and window pier panels alike were painted conservative hunter green. Now every train on the New Haven from the *Merchants Limited* to a numbers-only Springfield local had the new *Shoreliner* cars in its consist.

In a tribute to thirsty New York commuters, the two tavern-observations built specially for the

Call Cards—To insure the discharge of passengers at stations to which they are destined, the conductor or employe in charge shall list the destination of each passenger on Form 93.820 "Destination and Breakfast Call Card" and place it in the receptacle provided therefore in the clean linen locker. Such listings shall be made in the order in which stations are reached and in time order according to the time the passenger wishes to be called. Information regarding the time the train is scheduled to reach the station listed and the number of persons occupying each accommodation shall also be shown on the Call Card in the space provided.

The conductor shall prepare and distribute the call card as soon as possible after departure from terminal and is responsible for keeping it "up to date" at all times. The porter must see that he receives a call card prepared for his car. He shall check the listings on the call card against the space occupied and if all passengers are not accounted for or if their destination seems to be incorrect, such inconsistencies must be called to the attention of the Pullman conductor.

In most instances the conductor obtains "calls" from passengers, however, on cars leaving late at night, while the conductor is checking passengers at table in station, the porter will ask passengers when they wish to be called and enter this information on the call card given to him by the conductor. Immediately after departure the conductor shall prepare a new call card listing calls taken by the porter. He shall check to see that a call has been taken for each passenger and that it is correct in accordance with destination of passenger.

The call card shall be kept in the linen locker receptacle until completion of trip when conductor will deposit it with earnings reports.

Occupancy of Cars in Stations after Arrival. Employes shall notify passengers of occupancy privileges where car is parked at station following early morning arrival. Inform passengers of the arrival time and how long they may remain in the car.

Where breakfast service is available on the train in the morning, advise passengers before they retire, and take calls according to their wishes.

Calling Passengers. Calls shall be made by the porter or employe relieving him. If call is for a definite time, such as 7:30 a.m., call the passenger at that time, regardless of whether the train is delayed. If call is for a certain amount of time before arrival, call the passenger the specified amount of time before arrival making allowance for train delay. When calling passengers, the porter must not part the berth curtains, or under any circumstances, place his hand inside the curtains.

Porter shall awaken passengers in lower berths by grasping the berth curtain at the head end of the berth and pushing gently under the mattress, at the same time saying in a low tone of voice, for example, "Good morning, lower 5, it is seven o'clock." Porters shall awaken passengers in upper berths by grasping the curtain at the head end of the bed, pulling it taut and tapping it. If necessary, curtain may be pulled sideways to gather surplus and the mattress pushed gently from outside the curtain. Upper berth passengers shall also be called quietly and advised of the time. Awaken passengers in rooms by use of the buzzer or door knocker. In all cases, the employe shall continue to call passengers until they respond. Employes shall explain to room passengers before they retire that answer to call may be made by pressing the call button or knocking on the door. If railroad furnishes information regarding temperature and weather conditions, passengers must also be given this information at the time the call is made. Employe, at an opportune time, shall always make polite inquiry of passengers as to how they rested.

The conductor and porter jointly are responsible for seeing that passengers are discharged at correct destination. The conductor shall call the attention of the porter or attendant to any passengers who will leave the train at stations short of terminal or under unusual circumstances.

During the day, porters shall locate passengers at least 10 minutes before arrival at destination; at night and in the early morning, passengers shall be called in accordance with the time designated on the call card.

When approaching terminals or important stations where several passengers are to be detrained the conductor or employe assigned to the car shall announce the station and designate end of car from which passengers will leave.

At intermediate stations ascertain from train conductor if car will reach station platform for discharge of passengers. If not, notify train conductor and arrange for discharge of passengers from car alongside platform.

Train conductors shall be notified in advance of all cases where passengers will need wheelchairs or ambulances so that they may be ordered.

Local regulations regarding the location of employes when discharging passengers at terminals must be respected.

The conductor and porter or attendant who, because of negligence or for other reasons, detrain passengers or their luggage at other than their correct destination, shall make a detailed report, giving all facts to district representative upon completion of trip.

Conductors shall look through cars in their charge at the end of trip to make sure all passengers are off and that lost property is cared for.

In 1952 the Pullman Company published a small black book entitled Instructions to Porters, Attendants and Bus Boys. In it were these instructions.

---

premier *Merchants Limited* were relegated to New Haven-New York commuter service by the early 1950s. Their expansive tavern-lounge was apparently put to much greater use in that concentrated marketplace.

People-pleasing car features included Sleepy Hollow seats, automatic doors, bright fluorescent lighting for the color coordinated interiors, outside swing hanger trucks for a silken ride and five-foot-wide panoramic windows. Some cars even carried day roomettes and drawing rooms. The only available radio-telephone service on the Shoreliner fleet was on the *Merchants,* and the joint NH/PRR Boston-Washington *Senator.* The Shoreliner fleet carried NH passengers through the Penn Central era into Amtrak, and local Boston commuters until the late 1980s.

YOUR FAVORITE ARMCHAIR ON WHEELS, THE B&O REVISITED

Soon the line between streamliners purchased "out of the box" and new services created with rebuilt older equipment began to blur. No finer example of this blending of new and old was found than the Baltimore & Ohio's *Cincinnatian,* inaugurated on January 19, 1947.

Between 1946 and 1953, the Baltimore & Ohio spent much more on new equipment than it did on road improvements. In both 1947 and 1948, more than $40 million was spent on new equipment, although the B&O's investment in passenger equipment was modest. New equipment purchased from EMC in 1937 prior to the war included #51 and #52, each 3,600-hp A-B diesel units that were to be separated only for servicing and maintenance. EMD

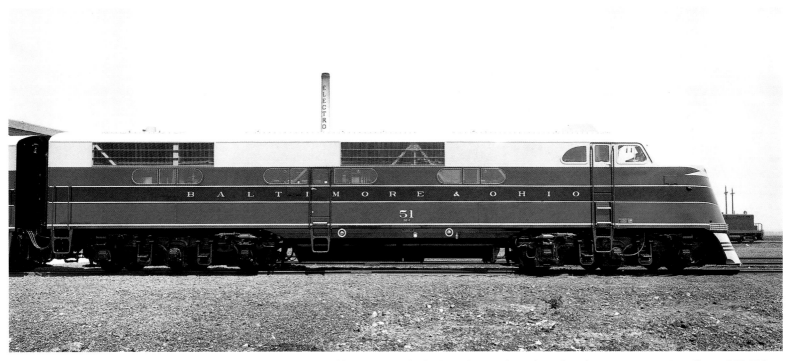

Profile view of #51A reveals its sleek lines and smooth styling. The unit weighed 329,000 pounds and produced a starting tractive effort of 55,850 pounds. EMD

Royal Blue — B. & O. R. R., Diesel-Powered Streamlined Train between Washington and New York

The B&O's Royal Blue *streamliner between New York and Washington provided the latest features in travel comfort including air-conditioning and telephones, free reserved seats, coffee shop, dining car, drawing-room parlor car and a cafe-lounge observation car. Dick Bowers*

A Baltimore & Ohio stainless steel sleeper gets the finishing touches like lettering applied in the Budd plant. In 1951 the B&O took in $26 million in passenger revenues and totaled 799 million passenger-miles. In the summer of 1954, eleven new duplex roomette-bedroom sleepers were added to the Capitol Limited, *the* National Limited *and the* Diplomat. *Budd*

Scheduled to cover the 570 miles between its namesake city and Baltimore in 12 1/2 hours, the *Cincinnatian* was an all-day coach-only train with service via Washington and 10 other stops. Average speed was about 45 mph, but crossing the Allegheny Mountains, coupled with the various slowdowns and station stops, put a premium on the locomotive's ability to quickly slow down, then accelerate back to speed.

Constructed from 10 old heavyweight cars and four 1927 Presidents Class 4-6-2 Pacific locomotives, the *Cincinnatian* was B&O's first postwar streamliner. Unless having seen the transformation taking place at the B&O's Mount Clare Shops, the average passenger could not detect any indication that the train had not just arrived from one of the big three carbuilders.

Behind the streamlined steam locomotive—one of which had been streamlined in 1937-38 for *Royal Blue* service and then had same removed—came the baggage-buffet-lounge, three coaches and a dining-observation car.

The Dining Car on this Train Has a

Place Set for You

Add to the enjoyment of your trip by having a delicious meal prepared by skilled chefs and served by courteous waiters.

$2.45

PANNED SEASONAL FISH, TARTAR SAUCE

FRIED POTATOES

BREAD   BUTTER   SALAD BOWL

COFFEE, TEA OR MILK

$2.45

CREAMED HAM AND TURKEY ON TOAST

SALAD BOWL

BREAD   BUTTER

COFFEE, TEA OR MILK

Present this in Dining Car. We will be happy to assist you in your selection.

BALTIMORE AND OHIO RAILROAD

J. B. Martin,
Manager, Dining Car and
Commissary Department
Baltimore & Ohio R. R.
Baltimore 1, Maryland

5-6-M-8-2

"Add to the enjoyment of your trip by having a delicious meal prepared by skilled chefs and served by courteous waiters," read the B&O meal card.

The daily Royal Blue *ran between Jersey City, Philadelphia, Wilmington, Baltimore and Washington. In 1948 its New York Central bus connection left New York City's 42nd Street Bus Station at 8:45 a.m. via the Holland Tunnel, while the train arrived in Washington at 2 p.m. Continuing west using connecting trains, travelers would arrive in Chicago the next morning at 7 a.m. Central Standard Time.*

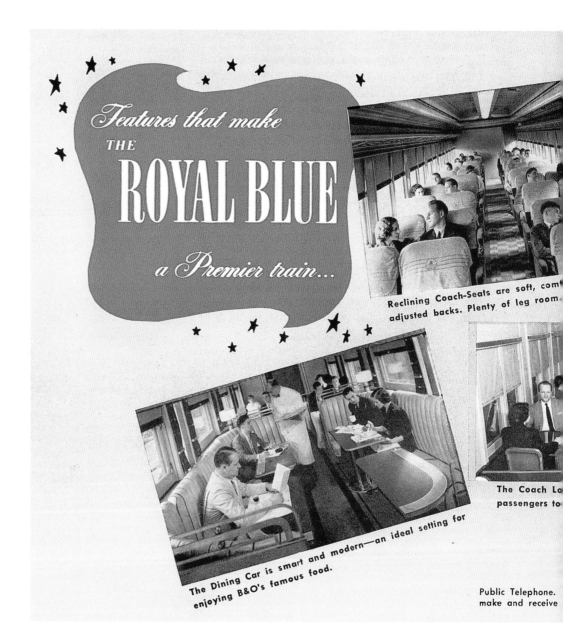

Features that make

THE

ROYAL BLUE

a Premier train...

Reclining Coach-Seats are soft, comf adjusted backs. Plenty of leg room.

The Dining Car is smart and modern—an ideal setting for enjoying B&O's famous food.

The Coach Lo passengers to

Public Telephone. make and receive

Interior appointments included marlite paneling of various colors, but B&O blue and cream predominated with stainless steel trim and accents. Coach seating was the Sleepy Hollow type, with upholstered sofas and chairs filling the observation section. Floors were tiled in various patterns except for the carpet in the observation. The dining section virtually sparkled, with gloss black floor tile, Persian red walls and leather

The flashing Jet Rocket *on the Rock Island replaced the Peoria Rocket—but only briefly in mid-1957—between Chicago and Peoria. Rock Island had several locomotives that were an off-beat and unusual style.*

This 2,000-hp Alco-GE unit, built in 1941 and nicknamed Christine, *thanks to being repowered by EMD, eventually ended up being parted out for off-shore drilling rigs. Richard Wallin*

Rock Island #2 was a 1,200-hp GM-EMD LWT12 built in 1955. It was later donated to the National Railroad Museum in Green Bay, Wisconsin.

This full page full color ad appeared in Holiday *magazine heralding the arrival of the Rock Island's* Golden Rocket *between Chicago and Los Angeles. The train was to feature reclining seats, a lounge, diner, sleeping cars and an observation car with buffet and beverage service, barber shop and valet. Ironically the train was never placed in service, and the cars were assigned to the Golden State.*

Arriving soon...Rock Island's new super-luxury Rocket

The GOLDEN ROCKET

In only 39¾ hours this magnificent, million dollar train will whisk you between Chicago and Los Angeles!

'Most any day now, America's most beautiful new Diesel-electric train, the Golden Rocket, will begin 39¾-hour, super-de luxe service between Chicago and Los Angeles over the scenic Rock Island-Southern Pacific Golden State Route.

Riding the Golden Rocket will be a thrilling adventure; its decorations capture the picturesque beauty of the Southwest—the grandeur of its mountains, deserts and canyons—the inspiring colors of its flowers, minerals and native costumes.

The Golden Rocket strikes a high note in comfort and convenience. *Coach Passengers* enjoy deep-cushioned, form-fitting reclining seats with individual, full-length leg-rests. *The Fiesta Car*—gay meeting place for all passengers—has a refreshment bar, a coffee shop lounge, and a dining section serving delicious meals at modest prices. *The Diner* offers full-meal service comparable to that of the finest restaurants. *Sleeping cars* are all-room cars with roomettes, bedrooms, compartments and drawing rooms. *The Observation* has a fine lounge with buffet and beverage service, barber shop and valet.

For the utmost in travel luxury at modest extra fare, ride the Golden Rocket. Ask your local Rock Island Passenger Agent for full facts—or write: A. D. Martin, Passenger Traffic Manager, Rock Island Lines, 723 La Salle Street Station, Chicago 5, Illinois.

Rock Island

■ Golden State Route   ■ Other Rock Island Routes

The Golden Rocket travels the famous Golden State Route between Chicago and Los Angeles via Kansas City. Convenient connections with other Rock Island trains originating in the Twin Cities, St. Louis and Memphis.

Rock Island Lines
ROUTE OF THE ROCKETS

39-3266

RI #625 was a 2,000-hp E-3A built by GM-EMC in June/July of 1939 that featured classic lines and a beautiful paint scheme. EMD

When the Empire Builder (Chicago to Seattle/Portland) began service in 1947, it was train service at its very best. The train consisted of sleepers, coaches, baggage-mail, diner, coffee shop-kitchen-dormitory cars, and bed-room-lounge-sleepers. Decorated in Great Northern's bright orange and green, the air-conditioned cars were impressive and stylish. In 1951 the railroad added more cars to the Empire Builder for a total of $8.4 million.

THE *Empire Builder* — GREAT NORTHERN RAILWAY STREAMLINER

ALONG PUGET SOUND NORTH OF SEATTLE, WASH.   8B-H390

Newly-manufactured Great Northern diesel E units, built by EMD, sit on parallel tracks for a publicity photo. In 1949, the GN ordered 66 new passenger cars at a cost of $8.4 million for the Empire Builder.

EMPIRE BUILDER: JAMES J. HILL'S LEGACY

Of all the great streamliners, few caught the imagination of the general public like the *Empire Builder*. Ordered in late 1943, it was nearly 3 1/2 years before the equipment was ready to be presented to the public.

On a bright, brisk February 7, 1947 the city fathers of St. Paul and Minneapolis, accompanied by appropriate Great Northern officials, duly christened the *Empire Builder* as the first new postwar Western streamliner. For the following three weeks the streamliner made public appearances across the GN system, and finally entered service on February 27, 1947 when sets left Seattle and Chicago respectively.

Empire Builder service required five 12-car sets of equipment, one owned by partner CB&Q, which handled the train between Chicago and St. Paul, and the remaining four sets by the Great Northern.

James J. Hill was a railroad empire builder, and the Great Northern was the greatest of his railroads. Hill was a master of detail and had excellent command of many aspects of railroading. The strong foundation he built helped the GN in later years to purchase new diesel equipment, such as these brand new EMD 2,000-hp E-7s in 1945. EMD

Each 12-car set included a 60-seat coach, three 48-seat day-night Sleepy Hollow coaches, coffee shop-lounge-dormitory, dining car and five Pullmans including the lounge-observation. All equipment was built by Pullman-Standard, and twin EMD E-7's supplied the power (except through Cascade Tunnel where electrics reigned). Total capacity was 204 coach passengers and 101 sleeping car passengers.

In response to the traveling businessman, the Burlington added a parlor car to its portion of the westbound run, placing a stainless steel exclamation point right in front of the observation car in the otherwise solid orange and green streamliner.

Since this parlor car returned to Chicago on a *Zephyr*, the incongruity was never present on the eastbound *Builder*.

Inside, passengers found comfort and service galore. All coaches had coordinated pastel colors of blue, tan, green or yellow, plus air conditioning, and venetian blinds to shade the sun. First class passengers had a choice of accommodations, including traditional sections, duplex roomettes, bedrooms and even three-person drawing rooms.

The coffee shop-lounge and bedroom-buffet-observation cars were decorated with motifs from the Blackfoot Indians of the plains. Images includ-

60-PASSENGER COACH · RECLINING SEATS · FOOT RESTS

The Empire *Builder's* exhibition period was held February 6-19, 1947 in cities where the train would run. Travelers got to see a 60-seat coach with reclining seats.

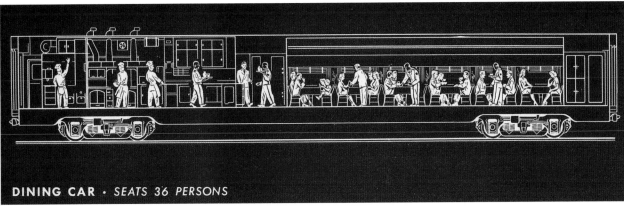

DINING CAR · SEATS 36 PERSONS

This dining car was a favorite place for many: unusually great steaks, chicken or beef, soups and salads, all with a friendly smile from the waiter.

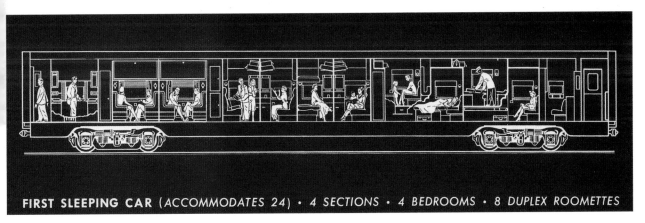

FIRST SLEEPING CAR (ACCOMMODATES 24) · 4 SECTIONS · 4 BEDROOMS · 8 DUPLEX ROOMETTES

Retiring at night meant having the porter make up the bed, and passengers rode comfortably, falling asleep with the clickety-clack of the rails.

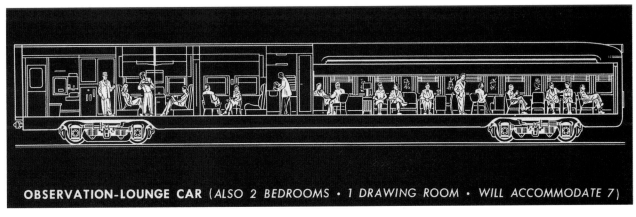

OBSERVATION-LOUNGE CAR (ALSO 2 BEDROOMS · 1 DRAWING ROOM · WILL ACCOMMODATE 7)

The end car, the observation, was meant for folks to gather and take in the sights along the right-of-way. Some, like this one, included several bedrooms.

Pullman-Standard's stake in railroading was huge. It produced hundreds of passenger cars and thousands of freight cars in its six manufacturing plants for the nation's railroads. This Saturday Evening Post ad explains the benefits of traveling via GN's Empire Builder.

NOW BUILDING BY
Pullman-Standard
FOR FASTER, FINER SERVICE TO THE PACIFIC NORTHWEST
GREAT NORTHERN'S NEW
Empire Builders

The first *Empire Builders* began de luxe service between Chicago, Minneapolis-St. Paul and the Pacific Northwest in 1929. They have a magnificent record. They were built by Pullman-Standard, world's leading car-builder. The new Empire Builders, comprising Sleeping Cars, Diners, Coffee Shop Cars and Coaches, now building by Pullman-Standard, are "Trains of Tomorrow" in every detail of engineering, design and construction.

Cutting many hours off present schedules, these will be the first streamlined, all-accommodation trains to serve the Northwest border territory. Mark your travel calendar to ride these new trains from Chicago West . . . along the colorful route whose distances unfold the panorama of the Blackfeet Indian country and the grandeur of the Montana Rockies in Glacier National Park.

For the *safest* and *finest* in modern transportation, travel on cars and trains built by Pullman-Standard. Their quality combines the latest in styling and design with a structural soundness—a car-building know-how—derived from having built most of America's best cars. The Pullman-Standard nameplate on any railway car is your assurance of this quality.

The Coffee Shop Car, decorated in Blackfeet tribal symbols, will adjoin the coach section of the new Empire Builders, for the convenience of passengers who prefer light lunches to full-course meals.

© P-S. C. M. CO.

Pullman-Standard CAR MANUFACTURING COMPANY
CHICAGO • ILLINOIS Offices in seven cities . . . Manufacturing plants in six cities
World's largest builders of modern streamlined railroad cars

LEFT. The deluxe all-Pullman Panama Limited of Illinois Central was a sleek, streamlined chocolate brown and orange passenger train that ran between Chicago and New Orleans. The picture shows an almost cozy winter scene in the Windy City of Chicago, probably in the l950s. Jay Christopher BELOW. The cover of the IC's on-board beverage list matched the colors of the exterior of the passenger cars. In this 1969 version, a cocktail was about $1.00, with beer and ale, $.55. Wines and liqueurs were about $1.00 as well.

IC's passenger department was large and influential during and after World War II. An IC ad in 1944 read in part, "Thanks to the IC family spirit, we have made the best of another war-time difficulty. After victory, all that our workers have learned in the war years will be turned to improving IC (passenger) service. We want to keep on earning your good will."

MICHIGAN AVENUE SKYLINE, CHICAGO

ILLINOIS CENTRAL — *Main Line of Mid-America*

'Ambassador of Good Will'
—*That's Dining Service*

"Recently I had the rare pleasure of traveling on your City of New Orleans. The food service, in terms of variety, quantity and quality, still leaves me wondering as to just how you manage to do it."—R. L. Rivers, Amherst, Mass.

TO LEARN how the Illinois Central manages to do it, Mr. Rivers would have to take a behind-the-scenes look at the dining service department's everyday activities. In doing so, he would find the reason why such service is typical. Primarily it is the mixing of many ingredients, such as careful training and instruction of personnel, teamwork, high morale, and a calculated concern for details.

To serve approximately one-and-one-third million meals, as it did last year, is something the department takes in stride. But to prepare and serve those meals in such a fashion that they elicit responses like that from Mr. Rivers, and many others, is one of the prime objectives of the department.

"In serving that many meals on our 21 scheduled passenger trains and in our restaurant at Central Station, Chicago, we like to think that we have made many friends for the railroad," says Paul E. Bickenbach, general superintendent dining service. In fact, all 500 members of the department consider making enthusiastic and lasting friends for the railroad as one of their most important jobs.

TOP, LEFT. Scenes like this show IC's graceful passenger trains with the magnificent Michigan Avenue skyline of Chicago in the background. TOP, RIGHT. The King's Dinner *was a delight to behold—and IC meal service consisted of fresh white linen table-cloths and napkins, polished silverware and heavy china. LEFT. The IC's employee magazine hints at the pride the company took in its dining service.*

RIGHT. In l948, IC's Panama Limited *consisted of only Pullman cars, a single parlor car and a diner. The train was completely air conditioned, featured a radio and valet service. The name* Panama Limited *was even stenciled on the front of the powerful diesel locomotive. EMD BELOW, LEFT. Mrs. Casey Jones is flanked by IC conductor E. E. Jolly and Engineer William Boedeke in this shot taken next to IC's 1941-built E-6A passenger diesel.*

TRAIN PORTER'S   CLAIM CHECK

PANAMA LIMITED

Car Number_____

Date_____

Destination - TAXICAB STAND

At   NEW ORLEANS, LA.

ILLINOIS CENTRAL

FORM GPO-119

93968

PASSENGER'S CLAIM CHECK

Car Number_____

Date_____

Liability Limited to $50.00 on each Article, except as provided by Tariff.

Present this check to Red Cap at taxicab stand at NEW ORLEANS Station.

ILLINOIS CENTRAL

93968

FORM GPO-119

PREVAILING RED CAP SERVICE FEE PAYABLE UPON DELIVERY OF YOUR BAGGAGE.

LEFT. The Skytop parlor-observation lounge cars on the Milwaukee Road were designed by Brooks Stevens and were described as "the finishing touch to a perfect train." The cars were built by the railroad's own shops. At the rear, three rows of large glass windows were stacked atop each other so that passengers looking skyward would have an excellent view of city skyscrapers or country clouds. Owen Leander BELOW. Dome travel was promoted as "the way to go" on the Milwaukee Road, especially because of the spectacular territory through which the train ran. Russ Porter

This is the interior of a Milwaukee Road Skytop lounge observation car looking towards the front of the car, with the more impressive solarium portion of the car at the rear. Passengers could sit and talk, watch the scenery or sip a drink as the train sped toward its destination. Owen Leander

The January 4, 1995 obituary of Brooks Stevens as announced by the Associated Press in the Chicago Tribune.

Industrial designer Brooks Stevens, 83

ASSOCIATED PRESS

MILWAUKEE—Brooks Stevens, whose streamlined designs were expressed in everything from Studebakers and Harley-Davidsons to lawn mowers, passenger trains and a fiberglass "weinermobile," died Wednesday. He was 83.

The Milwaukee native was credited for producing industrial designs for 585 companies throughout the world in a career that started in 1933.

His automotive designs included a civilian version of the Jeep, and later Jeep station wagons and the Jeep Cherokee.

Mr. Stevens also designed sky-top lounge railroad cars for Milwaukee Road and tractors for Allis-Chalmers that he said were so popular that some farmers drove them to church.

Another of his favorites was the "wienermobile," a vehicle with a fiberglass body in the shape of a hot dog used as a promotional tool for Oscar Mayer.

THE DIESEL-POWERED, STREAMLINED NORTH COAST LIMITED

The colorful streamlined passenger trains of the Northern Pacific began showing up on company property after it purchased new equipment in 1946 from the Pullman-Standard Company. In 1954 the train and its interior was redesigned by Raymond Loewy, including its rich two-tone green exterior paint scheme. The North Coast Limited *enjoyed a good run, passing more than two dozen mountain ranges along its Chicago to Portland/Seattle route.*

"A friendly, courteous steward welcomes you to the new, beautifully-appointed dining car on the Vista-Dome North Coast Limited. *The car seats 32 in the main central section and eight in each of two glass-partitioned banquettes," reads the Northern Pacific promotion.*

NORTH COAST LIMITED:
NORTHERN PACIFIC'S FLAGSHIP

Within weeks of the *Olympian Hiawatha's* introduction, parallel Northern Pacific fielded its streamliner masterpiece, the *North Coast Limited.* Nudged on by Milwaukee and GN competition, the NP placed its train into service before all the new equipment was delivered.

Back on November 28, 1946 the NP, Burlington, and SP&S had initialed purchase orders for $9.3 million to acquire a total of 78 cars from Pullman-Standard and six 3-unit locomotives from EMD. Ten of those cars were ordered by the Burlington for its share of the Chicago-Seattle

ABOVE. Passing Savanna, Illinois along the Mississippi River, the observation car of the North Coast Limited *looks warm and inviting in this December, 1966 scene. Chris Burritt*

market, and little SP&S ordered two cars for its Portland section. Six sets were required for daily operation, and each nominally ran 16 cars. Equipment was delivered piecemeal, and locomotives, coaches, lounges and diners were individually integrated into the operating *North Coast Limited* consist. Finally, all was streamlined except for the sleepers, so standard Pullmans were painted in matching two-tone green to substitute for the as yet undelivered streamlined replacements.

Although slower than the *Empire Builder*, the *North Coast Limited* was stiff competition. Proudly displaying its Loewy two-tone green exterior, and the likes of big baked Idaho potatoes as

NEXT PAGE, BOTTOM. *Luxury trains with all sorts of amenities were making headlines weekly as travel after World War II encouraged railroads to upgrade their equipment. "Lewis & Clark Traveller's Rest buffet-lounge car and a helpful, friendly Stewardess-Nurse are extras which add to your pleasure on the Vista-Dome North Coast Limited..." boasted the NP. TOP. EMD-built SF-1 and SF-2 diesels powered the sleek* City of San Francisco *on the Union Pacific. Note the rounded porthole-type windows and the rounded nose of the diesel; even the coupling between the units was made as streamlined as possible. EMD*

The *Vista-Dome* North Coast Limited opens a new panorama of scenic beauty to travelers in the Northern Pacific West

The Club Car Lounge on the City of San Francisco was colorful and inviting. The train didn't charge any extra fare for its amenities.

In this 1955 brochure, the Milwaukee Road-Union Pacific-Southern Pacific said the City of San Francisco was not only the finest but the fastest train between Chicago and the train's namesake: westbound the train departed Chicago in early evening and arrived the second morning.

ABOVE. These UP diesels
were E-6s built before the
war in 1940; after 1946 they
were renumbered; they were
rated at 2,000 hp. EMD

part of the sumptuous meals in its diner, thousands of satisfied customers rode it yearly. The *North Coast* kept up the good fight until Amtrak, with some of the last and finest equipment and service innovations the late 1950s could devise.

THE *CITIES* EXPAND: UNION PACIFIC EXTENDS ITS FLEET

On February 15, 1947 the Union Pacific had adequate equipment in the *City* pool with the Chicago & North Western to place the *City of Portland* in daily operation, and the *City of Los Angeles* followed on May 14. Working with partner Southern Pacific, on September 1, 1947 the *City of San Francisco* likewise became a daily train.

The daily operation of the *City* fleet was no small accomplishment. The *City of Portland* had four 10-car sets and one of nine cars. The *City of San Francisco* had four 14-car sets, and the *City of Los Angeles* two sets of 12 cars and two of 13 cars. Thus, a total of more than 150 cars were required, including cars rotated out for maintenance. It was a stunning accomplishment for the Overland Route.

Streamliner **CITY OF LOS ANGELES**
BETWEEN CHICAGO, OMAHA AND LOS ANGELES
Daily Service
Extra Fine——Extra Fast——Extra Fare
All Schedules Are Shown in Standard Time

Elev.	Miles	PLACE	Chicago to Los Angeles Extra Fare (Read Down)	Los Angeles to Chicago Extra Fare (Read Up)
		C. & N. W.	No. 103	No. 104
590	0	CHICAGO...(Central Time).....Ill.	Lv. 6:15 pm	Ar. 9:45 am
598	138	Clinton....................Iowa	Lv. 8:29 pm	Ar. 7:10 am
731	219	Cedar Rapids................. "	Lv. 9:40 pm	Ar. 5:55 am
917	327	Ames....................... "	Lv. 11:13 pm	Ar. ♦ 4:20 am
1138	340	Boone..................... "	Lv. 11:35 pm	Ar. 4:02 am
1033	488	Omaha...................Neb.	Ar. 2:00 am	Lv. 1:50 am
		Union Pacific		
1033	488	OMAHA...................Neb.	Lv. 2:10 am	Ar. 1:40 am
1197	525	Fremont.................... "	Lv.♦ 2:43 am	Lv.♦ 1:00 am
1447	570	Columbus................... "	Lv.♦ 3:16 am	Lv.♦12:22 am
1864	632	Grand Island............... "	Lv. 4:10 am	Lv. 11:31 pm
2149	674	Kearney (State Normal)........ "	Lv.♦ 4:44 am	Lv.♦10:51 pm
2802	769	North Platte (Central Time).... "	Ar. 5:55 am	Lv. 9:38 pm
2802	769	North Platte (Mountain Time).. "	Lv. 5:00 am	Ar. 8:33 pm
4091	893	Sidney..................... "	Lv. 6:43 am	Lv. 6:52 pm
6060	995	Cheyenne (Capital of Wyoming).Wyo.	Ar. 8:25 am	Lv. 5:30 pm
6060	995	Cheyenne (Fort Warren)....... "	Lv. 8:35 am	Ar. 5:20 pm
7151	1051	Laramie (State University).... "	Lv. 9:55 am	Lv. 4:10 pm
6747	1168	Rawlins (State Penitentiary).... "	Lv. 11:40 am	Lv. 2:20 pm
6083	1302	Green River (Water flows to "	Ar. 1:50 pm	Lv. 12:05 pm
6083	1302	Green River (Gulf of California) "	Lv. 2:00 pm	Ar. 11:55 am
6745	1402	Evanston..................Wyo.	Lv. 3:40 pm	Lv. 10:14 am
4298	1478	Ogden (Junction with So. Pac.)..Utah	Lv. 5:25 pm	Lv. 8:45 am
4251	1514	Salt Lake City (State Capital).. "	Ar. 6:10 pm	Lv. 7:50 am
4251	1514	Salt Lake City.............. "	Lv. 6:20 pm	Ar. 7:40 am
4968	1721	Milford (Mountain Time)...... "	Lv. 9:30 pm	Lv. 4:37 am
2027	1964	Las Vegas (Pacific Time).....Nev.	Ar. 1:15 am	Lv. 10:55 pm
2027	1964	Las Vegas (Hoover Dam)...... "	Lv. 1:25 am	Ar. 10:45 pm
1076	2229	San Bernardino...............Cal.	Ar. 6:20 am	Lv. 5:38 pm
868	2240	Riverside.................. "	Ar.♦ 6:45 am	Lv.♦ 5:13 pm
161	2292	East Los Angeles............ "	Ar. 7:40 am	Lv. 4:20 pm
293	2299	LOS ANGELES.(Pacific Time).Cal.	Ar. 8:00 am	Lv. 4:00 pm
400	★ 7.0	Alhambra....................Cal.	Ar.★ 8:05 am	Lv.★ 3:25 pm
830	★ 9.8	Pasadena.................. "	Ar.★ 8:20 am	Lv.★ 3:10 pm
430	★ 18.6	Glendale.................. "	Ar.★ 8:40 am	Lv.★ 2:40 pm
400	★ 23.4	Anaheim.................. "	Ar.★ 8:50 am	Lv.★ 2:45 pm
35	★ 23.3	Long Beach................ "	Ar.★ 8:35 am	Lv.★ 2:50 pm
20	★ 33.3	San Pedro (Pacific Time).......Cal.	Ar.★ 9:05 am	Lv.★ 2:15 pm

♦ Conditional Stop—Consult Agent or Conductor.
★ Motor Bus connection at East Los Angeles; mileage is from East Los Angeles.

DOMELINER "CITY OF PORTLAND—CITY OF DENVER" IN THE COLUMBIA RIVER GORGE

UNION PACIFIC RAILROAD COLORPHOTO

The City of Portland *Domeliner skirts the Columbia River Gorge. The striking deep, rich yellow passenger cars and locomotives of the UP were favorites of many.*

Style and service were back, with full dining cars, lounge cars, sleepers of all descriptions and even observations cars. Although the streamliner fleet generally rolled behind Electro-Motive diesels, UP's magnificent 4-8-4 Northerns could and did handle them with beauty and efficiency. Alco occasionally supplied the power with its new streamlined 2,000-hp PA locomotive. Let the good times roll, and on the UP they did.

Needless to say, the Santa Fe with its every-other-day *Super Chief* and *El Capitan* was chomping at the bit. Regular phone calls went out to Budd to "hurry up!"

KANSAS CITY TO ST. LOUIS VIA WABASH

The Wabash wrapped up 1947 with a blue, grey and silver streamliner, installed on the Kansas City to St. Louis run in late November. Complementing the joint Wabash/UP *City of St. Louis* service, the *City of Kansas City* included a single EMD E-7, and ACF supplied the full bag-

"City of San Francisco" in the High Sierra

3B-H734

The City of San Francisco *(top) and the* City of Portland *were both elegantly-appointed Union Pacific passenger trains. The UP made sure their trains were advertised and noticed, annually releasing thousands of color postcards depicting their trains.*

Locomotive #962, a 2,400-hp E-9, pulls its Union Pacific passenger train into an adobe-style station in the Southwest. The people in the picture were all "staged."

The Union Pacific at one time even operated bus routes to help fill the voids where their tracks didn't run. Here at the East Los Angeles station, buses operated to Alhambra, Pasadena, Glendale, Whittier, Fullerton, Anaheim, Lakewood, Long Beach, Wilmington and San Pedro.

UNION
PACIFIC
RAILROAD

Here it is!

The <u>first</u> and <u>only</u> DOME DINING CAR

between **CHICAGO** • **LOS ANGELES** and **PORTLAND**

You'll find it a new and thrilling experience to dine in splendor while viewing the beauty of the scenic West. One vast, colorful panorama replaces another while your Domeliner speeds quietly over smooth-as-glass rails.

In this Astra Dome dining car, Union Pacific introduces innovations such as wide, clear-view windows and double-capacity air conditioning.

There is also a downstairs dining room with unusual color and charm. Secluded from this main dining room, is a delightful smaller room available for private parties.

★ ★ ★

When arranging a trip between Chicago and the Pacific Coast, ask to be routed on the "City of Los Angeles" or "City of Portland" Domeliners. There's *no extra fare.*

The richly appointed private dining room is really a "show piece."

• Enjoy the finest in relaxing rail travel and wonderful meals, graciously served. On arrival you can drive a new car provided by Hertz Rent-a-Car service. Rates are reasonable and include insurance coverage. Your car can be reserved in advance.

UNION PACIFIC RAILROAD
OMAHA 2, NEBRASKA

Dick Bowers

93

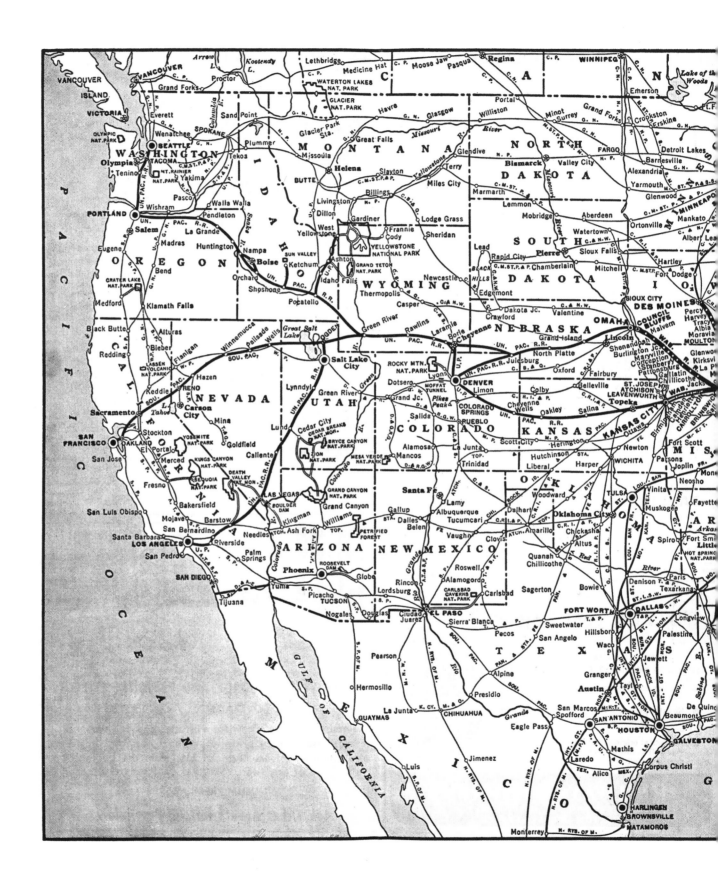

Decatur, Illinois was a division point on the Wabash, where passenger trains from St. Louis, Chicago and Detroit all stopped to load and unload passengers. Collection of Louis Marre

One of Wabash's few dome cars sits at Chicago in July of 1966, along with other Wabash varnish. Owen Leander

The Chicago, Burlington &
Quincy was the first user of
dome cars, and here the
Zephyrs *pass one another
near the Mississippi River
bluffs in a picturesque scene.*

VISTA DOME TWIN ZEPHYRS

TWICE DAILY VIA THE BURLINGTON BETWEEN CHICAGO AND ST. PAUL-MINNEAPOLIS

The Twin Cities Zephyr
*offered passengers radio
reception, a diner, parlor car
and, of course, a sleek way of
traveling. In addition, the
train was air-conditioned.
This publicity shot shows by-
standers admiring this sleek
new train. "If you happened
to see a Zephyr...in spectacular fashion it would flash by,
a mass of shimmering steel,
traveling a hundred miles an
hour," said CB&Q Superintendent E.F. Weber. Budd*

While passengers read, talked with other passengers or enjoyed the view, the diner's galley was busy preparing a delicious meal. Dinner in the diner was always a treat: meals were served using fine china and silverware, waiters were anxious to please and the food was as good as in a fancy restaurant. Cooks prepare a meal in the Twin Cities Zephyr kitchen. Budd

This map shows the routes of the Burlington Zephyrs that ran betwen Chicago-St. Louis-Minneapolis-Denver-Houston. Ten trains are shown in this routing map.

VISTA-DOMES VS SKYTOPS; CHICAGO-TWIN CITIES RIVALS

Another early Christmas present arrived on December 17, 1947 when the Burlington placed its new *Twin Cities Zephyr* in operation. The new 7-car Budd streamliner contained five dome cars. Behind twin EMD E-7's the consist included a baggage-club-lounge, four dome-coaches, diner and dome-parlor-observation. The first regularly scheduled vista-dome streamliner in service, the *Twin Cities Zephyr* drew record crowds and rave reviews.

Technical improvements included high-speed electro-pneumatic brakes, full-width diaphragms and 10-ton air conditioners. Each car withstood a 850,000-pound compression test with less than a 1/4 inch deflection.

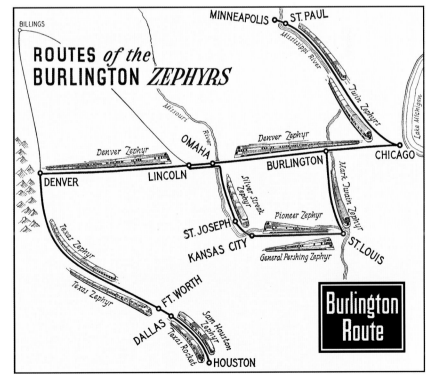

ROUTES *of the* BURLINGTON *ZEPHYRS*

Burlington Route

ABOVE AND LEFT. The styling of the Burlington Zephyrs and subsequent streamliner diesels was a matter of pride for the railroad. Locomotive #9911 was an EMC-built 2,000-hp E-5A constructed in 1940. There were even thin metal skirts fitted above the trucks and below the frame to hide some of the bulky sideframes. EMD

thank you...
For Purchasing Tickets
Via **BURLINGTON**

"YOU JUST CAN'T BEAT THE BURLINGTON FLEET!"

✻ DENVER ZEPHYR – Chicago-Denver-Colorado Springs

✻ TWIN ZEPHYRS – Chicago-St. Paul-Minneapolis

✻ CALIFORNIA ZEPHYR – Chicago-Denver-Salt Lake City-San Francisco

✻ KANSAS CITY ZEPHYR – Chicago-Kansas City

AMERICAN ROYAL ZEPHYR – Chicago-Kansas City

AK-SAR-BEN ZEPHYR – Chicago-Omaha-Lincoln

NEBRASKA ZEPHYR – Chicago-Omaha-Lincoln

TEXAS ZEPHYR – Dallas-Fort Worth-Denver

SAM HOUSTON ZEPHYR–Houston-Dallas-Fort Worth

BLACK HAWK – Chicago-St. Paul-Minneapolis

✻ EMPIRE BUILDER – Chicago-Twin Cities-Pacific Northwest

✻ NORTH COAST LIMITED – Chicago-Twin Cities-Yellowstone-Pacific Northwest

MAINSTREETER – Chicago-Twin Cities-Yellowstone-Pacific Northwest

WESTERN STAR – Chicago-Twin Cities-Glacier Park-Pacific Northwest

✻ *Featuring Vista-Dome Cars*

LEFT. The Burlington Rail-road issued this ticket holder which listed name CB&Q and other railroad passenger trains that connected with the CB&Q. The concept was to get passengers to accept the idea of being able to go any-where in the United States by train, whether it was by their railroad or another: the more passengers traveling the country, the more revenues the railroads would share in.

Interior color combinations varied in each car. Some examples were Indian red and orchid gray; soft brown and pastel green; turtle egg gray and Indian red. The handrails on the stairway into the dome was Plexiglas and glowed with hidden illumination during evening hours. Each dome-coach held 54 passengers, with another 24 non-revenue dome seats.

The replaced 1936 semi-articulated equipment

ABOVE. This CB&Q E-8 was built in 1949-50 with a 2,250-hp rating. In its silver livery with safety striping on the nose to warn motorists of its coming, this passenger unit upheld a bold image for the railroad. EMD

This 2,000-hp E-5A was built by EMC in 1941, and was rostered with the Colorado & Southern Railway, a subsidiary of the Burlington, thus the same paint scheme as the CB&Q. As of July, 1972, the C&S had three of these passenger A units and a B unit of the E-5A configuration. Chris Burritt

THE NEBRASKA ZEPHYR...DAILY BETWEEN CHICAGO, OMAHA AND LINCOLN

did not face retirement. In a tribute to Budd's exceptional construction quality, after 11 years, 2 million passengers and 3 million passenger-miles each, they were refurbished and continued in service as the *Nebraska Zephyrs*. Planned obsolescence was an unknown term to the craftsmen of both Budd and Burlington.

Responding as quickly as its shops and contracts with Pullman-Standard allowed, in early 1948 the Milwaukee Road began to re-equip its wartime *Hiawatha* fleet. More coaches, parlors, diners and lounges rolled from the company shops in West Milwaukee, but the best was literally saved for last.

Finally, the Milwaukee shops delivered the Skytop parlor-observations for the *Twin Cities Hiawatha*. With an observation lounge virtually identical to the transcontinental *Olympian Hiawatha,* but with 24 parlor seats replacing the sleeping accommodations, the Milwaukee Road had an observation car without peer. With the addition of Pullman-built super domes in 1952, the *Hiawatha* continued to hold forth against all comers in the Twin Cities-Chicago market until Amtrak. Ultimately, the Milwaukee handled more patrons on the route than its competitors.

Burlington's Nebraska Zephyr *provided fast, daytime service between Chicago, Omaha and Lincoln with accommodations such as an observation-parlor car, lounge, diner, coaches, a dinette-coach and a cocktail lounge. The train left Chicago at 12:30 p.m., arrived Omaha at 9 p.m. and arrived in Lincoln at 10:15 p.m.*

The rear observation car of the Nebraska Zephyr *with its wide and deep windows provided great viewing for passengers as they were hurled along on steel rails through corn country. Don Heimburger*

105

When the first Hiawatha appeared on May 29, 1935, it signaled a new era for train speed and travel. Milwaukee Road's Hiawathas covered Chicago to Minneapolis (Morning and Afternoon Hiawathas) and Minocqua (North Woods Hiawatha) and Chicago to Omaha and Sioux Falls (Midwest Hiawatha). Jim Scribbins, noted Hiawatha historian, has said, "No better name could have been chosen, no finer trains operated. The Hiawatha earned a reputation and a following that would have dumbfounded its creators." Extensive display of the new Hiawatha train was arranged, with nearly 140,000 people coming out to view it.

LEFT. Santa Fe's locomotive facilities in the late 1940s still has remnants of steam, but diesels such as the powerful 2,000-hp PA-ls built in 1946 were beginning to take over the chores. BELOW. Ready for its 39 3/4 hour trip to Chicago, the Super Chief, the flagship of the Santa Fe streamliners, is at Los Angeles Union passenger terminal prior to its 8 p.m. departure.

THE
KATY
RAILROAD

Timetables and advertisements reflect the "romance of the rails" that was prevalent during the l940s and 1950s, but already riding the rails was dying a slow death.

JULY 1, 1951

KANSAS
CITY
SOUTHERN
Lines

Southern Belle

STREAMLINED HOSPITALITY

DIESEL POWERED

KANSAS CITY-FLORIDA SPECIAL

Frisco's popular train between Kansas City and the Southeast

In addition to Diesel power and time-saving schedules, the Kansas City-Florida Special offers...

- Streamlined sleeping-cars with roomettes, bedrooms and bedroom suites thru to Miami . . . Berths, too
- Berths, bedrooms, roomettes and compartment to Jacksonville
- Streamlined reclining chair car thru to Jacksonville
- Lounge and dining car service

The Kansas City-Florida Special is the only thru train between Kansas City, Birmingham, Atlanta and Florida.

AND TO OKLAHOMA AND TEXAS—THE STREAMLINED, DIESEL-POWERED

METEOR
Between ST. LOUIS, TULSA and OKLAHOMA CITY

TEXAS SPECIAL
Between ST. LOUIS, DALLAS, FT. WORTH and SAN ANTONIO

THE SOUTHWEST'S OWN: THE KATY AND FRISCO FLYERS

Regional carriers Missouri-Kansas-Texas, universally known as the Katy, and St. Louis-San Francisco, called the Frisco, joined together for postwar Texas and Oklahoma service. Together they ordered eight EMD E-7 locomotives and 52 stainless steel sheathed cars from Pullman-Standard.

Between May 14-16, l948 the *Meteor* and jointly-operated *Texas Special* were inaugurated. The *Meteor* covered St. Louis to Oklahoma City via Tulsa, while the *Texas Special* rolled between San Antonio and St. Louis. The new trains were eyecatching. The stainless steel car sides were highlighted with a bright red window band and maroon underbody skirts which were offset with aluminum painted trucks. The bright red locomotives had the respective train name painted on their noses, while the *Texas Special* units even had complementary stainless steel fluting on the locomotive's lower sides.

Service included through Pullmans to New York and Washington via either the B&O or PRR. The finest interior design and impeccable service kept customers coming until the jet and interstates of the future.

This 2,000-hp E-7 A-A diesel unit was built by EMD in 1947 to handle the Texas Special *which ran between St. Louis and San Antonio under a pooling arrangement with the Frisco and the Katy railroads.*

Grand Canyon weekend

First day

Lv. Los Angeles. 1:30 p.m.
    Santa Fe Grand Canyon.

Second Day

Ar. Grand Canyon . . . . 7:00 a.m.
Lv. Grand Canyon . . . . 8:00 p.m.
    Change to sleeper at Ash Fork, 11:40 p.m.

Third day

Ar. Phoenix. . . . . 8:30 a.m.
Lv. Phoenix. . . . . 8:35 a.m.
    Southern Pacific Sunset Limited

Ar. Los Angeles . . . . 4:30 p.m.
Fare including tax: coach, $33.77; first class, $40.92

STANDARD tourist attraction of the Southwest, and well worth the title, is Grand Canyon. One of the more popular rest spots is Phoenix. Both can be combined in one easy roundtrip by rail from Los Angeles.

The through sleeper from Los Angeles arrives at Grand Canyon at 7 a.m., and it's less than a block walk to the awe-inspiring view at the rim. The Santa Fe agent will gladly fit you out with an all-expense-paid day including three meals at El Tovar Hotel and a morning and afternoon bus trip along the south rim. Before you get back on the train at 8 p.m. you will have a good but quick overall view of the canyon and a half hour or so of watching Hopi Indian dances.

The Grand Canyon-Phoenix run is on two trains, the *Grand Canyon* to Ash Fork, then in a sleeper off the *Chief* from Ash Fork to Phoenix. Because of this, you won't get to bed until after arrival in Ash Fork at 11:40 p.m.

It is not recommended that you confine your stay in Phoenix to the five minutes between the indicated arrival and leaving times. Phoenix is well worth a day or two of your vacation, although there may be a man with enough will power to continue without stopping over. If you plan to go on through, the two railroads use the same station.

The daylight return on the *Sunset Limited* combines a comfortable, distinguished train with the scenery of the Great American Desert, the Imperial Valley, and San Gorgonio Pass.

Niagara Falls honeymoon special

<table>
<tr><td colspan="2" align="center">Westbound</td><td colspan="2" align="center">Eastbound</td></tr>
</table>

Westbound		*Eastbound*	
Leave New York . . . . 9:00 a.m. <small>New York Central *Empire State Express*</small>		Leave Chicago. 11:00 p.m. <small>Baltimore & Ohio *Shenandoah.* Carries dome sleeper on even days of month</small>	
Arrive Niagara Falls . . . . 6:11 p.m.		Arrive Washington . . . . 4:30 p.m. <small>Leave Washington for New York on any of seven trains, stops may be made as you wish at Baltimore and Philadelphia.</small>	
Leave Niagara Falls . . . . 8:22 p.m. <small>New York Central train connects with *North Shore Limited*</small>		Fare including tax: coach, $60.10; first class, $89.33	
Arrive Chicago . . . . 8:15 a.m.			

THE standard money-saving circle trip in the East has for many years been the New York-Chicago round trip via the Baltimore & Ohio through Washington one way and the New York Central through Niagara Falls the other way. This diverse route is sold at the same fare as a roundtrip via the shortest route. Businessmen use this combination to include Baltimore, Washington, Philadelphia, Buffalo, Cleveland and New York on the same trip west from Chicago. Tourists use it to see the nation's capital, Niagara Falls and the world's largest city.

Using the B&O for the eastbound trip gives the best daylight schedule over the Alleghenies and allows an arrival in New York on the ferry from Jersey City, definitely the most impressive way to approach the big city. Going around the circle in this direction also gives the best possible Hudson River trip on the New York Central, allowing a view of one of the world's most beautiful river valleys in the morning light, plus a look at the Mohawk River Valley in the early afternoon. Evening arrival sets the stage for a view of Niagara Falls by floodlight, perhaps from the Park Restaurant picture windows. You might want to return to Chicago next day by either of two routes.

Domeliners all the way

First day
Leave Chicago. . . . . 12:30 p.m.
  Burlington *Kansas City Zephyr*
Arrive Kansas City. . . . . 8:45 p.m.
Second Day
Leave Kansas City . . . . 7:01 a.m.
  Missouri Pacific, *Colorado Eagle*
Arrive St. Louis . . . . 12:01 p.m.
Third day
Leave St. Louis . . . . 8:55 a.m.
  Wabash Blue Bird
Arrive Chicago . . . . 2:05 p.m.
Fare including tax: coach, $26.34; first class, $34.01.

THE exciting new dimension that the vista dome adds to train travel can be enjoyed in the wide rolling country of the Midwest as well as among the canyons and peaks of the Rockies. Here, for instance, is a circle trip between Chicago and Kansas City using three railroads with dome cars all the way. Round-trip fares apply and are only $2.20 more coach, $2.85 more first class, than if the direct route were used in both directions.

Starting from Chicago, you ride Burlington's brand-new *Kansas City Zephyr* over the new Kansas City Short Cut. This route uses the Burlington's main stem to Galesburg, turns southwest through rough Mississippi Valley countryside, crosses the great river at Quincy, and then runs westward through the green hills of Missouri to the beginning of the new cutoff at Brookfield. The construction scars are still raw on the 71 miles of new railroad. The arrival in Kansas City will convince you that one of the finest ways to enter a city is in a dome at night.

Kansas City to St. Louis on the *Colorado Eagle* offers views of the Missouri River and more lush Midwestern countryside, proving again that the dome has a way of putting the traveler in the middle of the landscape rather than alongside it. Biggest highlights of the Wabash *Blue Bird* dome trip are the roundabout voyage out of St. Louis via Delmar and the arrival in Chicago.

ABOVE. With its long hood and snout protruding from the train shed at St. Louis, Missouri Pacific #41 soaks up the sun on this August day in 1969. The train will soon give two blasts on the horn and proceed to its next destination. Owen Leander LEFT. Playing cards from railroads have become collectible, especially if the cards are new or like-new.

With all this new equipment, interline sleeper service was offered between Houston or El Paso and/or New York and Washington via the B&O or PRR. The existing *Colorado Eagle* also received new sleepers and dome cars as well.

The bulk of MoPac/T&P equipment was built of aluminum by American Car & Foundry. Most of the sleepers were of Pullman-Standard manufacture, while the majority of dome coaches, plus a few regular coaches and sleepers came from Budd. Resplendent in the *Eagle* colors of cream and blue, and headed by either EMD E- or Alco PA-type locomotives, they were instantly popular. Car types included dormitory-coaches, grill-coaches, standard and divided coaches, deluxe coaches, dome coaches, diners, diner-lounges and sleepers of at least three different configurations.

ABOVE. A 2,250-hp PA-2 built in 1951, #8013 is shown brand new and ready for service. RIGHT. Passengers board the Missouri Pacific's Colorado Eagle *dome car bound for the West in this promotional picture. Budd*

From a half-century later vantage point, it is appropriate to look back at the accommodations made by a Southwest carrier to the realities of legal segregation. There were divided grill-coaches, with identical end seating sections separated by the grill itself. Likewise, a number of partitioned coaches were constructed, and if that in itself was insufficient, an additional group of cars were fitted with removable curtains to insure on-the-spot racial separation. It was taken for granted that *all* first class accommodations including sleeper, lounge and dining car space was white only. Occasionally colored were allowed at a few curtained-off tables in the dining car. Ability to pay did not enter into the matter.

Interior decorations were top shelf. Micarta and Formica were widely used for table and divider surfaces, while pastel colors were intermingled throughout the cars. Diners seated 44,

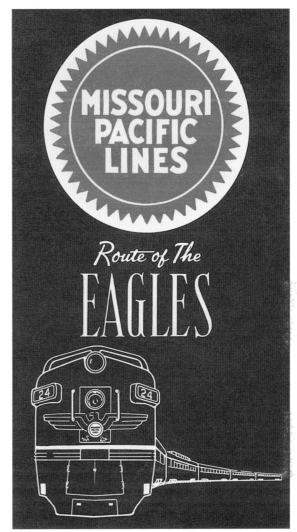

while diner-lounges seated 32 and 18 respectively. Fabrics varied from rust-colored mohair upholstery to canary yellow drapes. Various seating partitions ranged from wrought iron through Micarta to edge illuminated Plexiglas.

The dome coaches were the standard Budd design, and the sleepers a Pullman-Standard product. Interestingly, the coach patrons in the ACF cars had Heywood-Wakefield Sleepy Hollow seats to relax in, but the Budd dome coaches had the competitive Ride Master design from S. Karpen & Co.

All these new *Eagles* started or improved existing service on August 15, l948. A marked reduction in former running times also boosted patronage throughout the postwar era. The *Eagles* flew unimpeded until the jetliner clipped their wings two decades later.

ABOVE, LEFT. Looking westbound from the train station at Galva, Illinois, the overhead signals scream into the 2 a.m. darkness on Burlington's main line. Chris Burritt RIGHT. Coach seats on the popular Texas Eagles *were all reserved prior to boarding. The Eagle* included sleepers to a number of cities, a diner, parlor car and coaches.

With St. Louis as a convenient gateway to the West, Missouri Pacific used that fact as a promotional tool. The Eagle trains were served by some of the 66 diesel-electrics ordered by the MoPac in 1953 which brought the line closer to dieselization. By 1954, Mopac operated 819 diesels, using them on nearly 99% of the passenger trains they operated. With the 66 new diesels, MoPac's Texas and Louisiana lines were entirely operated by diesels, as was the Western District which extended into Kansas and Colorado.

MISSOURI PACIFIC LINES

ROUTE OF THE
Eagles

Issued April 25, 1954

USE THE ST. LOUIS GATEWAY

THE '48 *CENTURY:* FAVORITE TRAIN OF FAMOUS PEOPLE

The premier portion of New York Central's $86 million passenger car and service improvement program was to its flagship, the *20th Century Limited.* On September 15, 1948 the 260-foot red carpet was rolled out at Grand Central Terminal for the official inauguration of the new train. None other than General Dwight D. Eisenhower was guest speaker, at the time president of Columbia University. After a due christening with a champagne bottle filled with the waters of the Hudson and Lake Michigan, the 16-car train sets began their first revenue runs two days later.

No longer diffident about steam, management ordered matched EMD E-7 diesels for the new *Century.* Steam had been banished from the *Century* about 1947. Well aware of the encroachment of competition, NYC invested more than $4 million in the two trains and their power. Once again Dreyfuss was retained as designer.

First class service still held its legendary peak. A mid-train lounge offered not only drinks, but radio-telephone (no profanity allowed under violation of Federal law), and secretarial and/or valet services. A hot shower or shave was also available. Various configurations of all-room Pullmans made up the bulk of the train, but dining accommodations were special. A twin-unit diner-kitchen-dormitory car stretched 170 feet and seated 68 for dinner in one 85-foot car. The dormitory shared the second car with the kitchen and pantry areas. The observation-lounge had a raised Lookout Lounge in the rear, with floor-to-ceiling windows. Original artwork from a Manhattan gallery was on display and changed regularly. Patrons compared both the dining and lounge-observation cars to the finest clubs in Manhattan or Chicago.

The luxurious interiors included red leather sofas and grey leather upholstered chairs in the observation lounge. Flexwood filled the window pier panels and carpeting covered the floor. The focus of the lounge car lighting was a large wall mirror, thus visually doubling the size of the car. Specially designed lighting gave the effect of a floating luminous ceiling in these stunning cars. The floating ceiling concept was likewise carried into the dining car, where a vertical band of light-

New York Central was a leader in the movement of freight and passengers before it merged with the Pennsylvania Railroad on February 1, 1968 to form Penn Central. NYC's passenger trains dominated the eastern half of the United States, like the New England States at Beacon Park Yard. Leon Onofri, collection of Dick Bowers

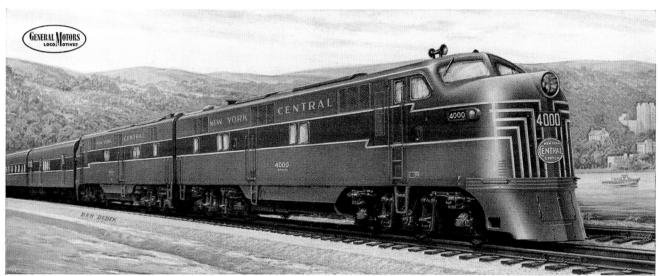

4000 H.P. DIESEL PASSENGER LOCOMOTIVE . . DESIGNED AND BUILT BY ELECTRO-MOTIVE DIVISION . . GENERAL MOTORS CORPORATION . . LA GRANGE, ILLINOIS, U. S. A.

Each of these 2,000-hp New York Central A-A units was equipped with two General Motors 12-cylinder V-type 2-cycle diesel engines. The locomotives were geared for a top speed of 98 mph; length over couplers was 142 feet for each pair.

ing separated the ceiling from the lower walls, creating the effect. Leather serpentine seats filled the center of the diner, with booth type facilities at each end. Its 85-foot length was divided into five distinct sections for either dining or lounging. No expense was spared, as Lucius Beebe claimed the floral bill for the *Century* as late as the early 1960s ran at over $1,000 per month.

Although the flagship of the postwar fleet, the *Century's* glamor lasted only a decade. Airliners by then were not only faster, but perceived as more glamorous. Worse, every mile of Central main line was now paralleled by interstate highway.

An era ended in April, 1958 when coaches were added to the all-Pullman train, much to the delight of Pennsy *Broadway Limited* clientele. A brief revival of days past occurred in the early 1960s, particularly with the addition of budget *Slumbercoach* accommodations. Unfortunately, the *20th Century Limited* faded away after a lin-

ABOVE. With its nameplate and number proudly displayed at the front of the locomotive, No. 4000 was a 2,000-hp E-7 built by EMD in 1945. It was one of eight such diesel units built in that year for the NYC. The diesel was painted in a two-tone gray with "lightning stripes" on the nose. EMD RIGHT. NYC #4018 leads a passenger train into an unknown station in later years, but prior to Amtrak. The telltale sign of the picture's vintage is the "cigar band" of white that extends around the nose of the unit. In 1967, the NYC showed numerous passenger trains still running over its line such as the Wolverine, Ohio State Limited, 20th Century Limited, James Whitcomb Riley, New England States, The Iroquois, the Laurentian *and others. Dick Bowers*

NEXT PAGE, TOP. New York Central's Hickory Creek *was a sleeper-buffet-lounge-observation car with wide rear windows. Here it's shown on the* 20th Century Limited *leaving Chicago in 1967. BOTTOM. Even in 1965, Chicago's train stations saw a lot of activity. A NYC train leaves Chicago's LaSalle Street Station. Both photos, Owen Leander*

We've got your *SLUMBER NUMBER* on the Water Level Route

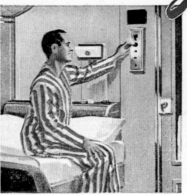

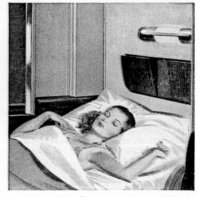

Is Climate your No. 1 slumber need?

For sound sleep, do you like a night that's mild as spring or brisk as autumn? Choose your own ideal slumber climate. A twist of your wrist controls the temperature of the clean, fresh, conditioned air in your New York Central room.

Does Privacy rate first with you?

Your room has its own complete toilet facilities... so take your time preparing for bed or getting ready for breakfast. Your room assures quiet privacy...so turn in early if you wish...and take your fill, too, of early morning sleep.

Or is your Bed most important?

Do you need a roomy, perfectly-made bed . : : with downy pillows, soft sheets and fluffy blankets tucked in around a mattress that's like a lullaby itself? You get them all...plus the gentlest of trips on the smooth *Water Level Route*.

Coming! **30 NEW DREAMLINERS!**

Central has ordered enough new, all-room sleeping cars to equip 30 new overnight *dreamliners!* Each has many *new* features, hand-picked by thousands of New York Central passengers...*plus* all the travel luxuries of the modern cars that already carry you swiftly, safely, with all-weather dependability over the *Water Level Route*.

NEW YORK CENTRAL The Water Level Route...You Can Sleep

This 1946 advertisement promoted the quiet ride passengers would get if they traveled via the New York Central. The "Water Level Route" meant smooth, level trackage for a comfortable ride. The ad also mentioned that new sleepers had been ordered that would equip 30 Dreamliners.

Owned and operated jointly by partners Burlington, Denver & Rio Grande Western and Western Pacific for a generation, the *California Zephyr* stood for all that was right and great about the American streamliner.

Budd built the equipment, Burlington led the promotion for it, and virtually all of America rode on it—or wanted to. When the collective soul-searching was completed by executives of WP, D&RGW and CB&Q, the purchase order to Budd was for 66 cars: 18 vista-dome coaches; eighteen 10-roomette/6-bedroom sleepers; six baggage cars, six diners, six vista-dome buffet-lounges, six

16-section sleepers and six vista-dome lounge-observations. The PRR purchased a 67th car, a 10-6 sleeper, for its transcontinental through sleeper service to New York (the NYC sometimes handled the car, but never purchased a specific *CZ* car for interline service).

Power was all diesel. The WP opted for EMD F units, as did the Burlington at first. Soon, however, the Q replaced the freight type units with their classic EMD E-7 or E-8 cabs. D&RGW chose Alco PA's—at least for the first years. Ultimately, the Rio Grande went to the EMD F unit for better traction on the front range of the Rockies.

NING CAR—so attractively decorated . . . spacious! Enjoy delicious food . . . meticu-
distinctive table appointments . . . the *Broadway Limited's* traditional touch at meal-
new kitchen car is adjoining—thus more table space . . . more comfort for dining.

DRAWING ROOMS—with complete facilities for three persons. Restful sofa and two folding easy chairs are replaced at night by the three beds shown above. Two wide windows . . . extra-large wardrobe . . . ample dressing space . . . enclosed toilet annex.

one or two persons,
mber-inviting lower
let annex. Adjoining
to one large room.

DUPLEX ROOMS—an upstairs-or-downstairs room — *something new* for the individual on the *Broadway Limited*. Full-length bed at night—a roomy daytime sofa. Handy writing table . . . complete toilet facilities.

NOW MORE OF THE POPULAR ROOMETTES—completely private for one person's comfort. An easy turn of a lever lowers your bed from the wall, replacing the restful daytime sofa-seat shown above. Enclosed wardrobe . . . panorama window . . . complete toilet facilities.

Dinner

$3.00

Please write on check each item desired; employees
forbidden to write meal checks or serve orders given orally.

Assorted Hors d'Oeuvres

Yankee Bean Soup   Hot Beef Broth   Chilled Tomato Juice
Iced Grapefruit Cocktail, Supreme

•

SELECT OYSTERS AU GRATIN IN CASSEROLE
OMELET WITH SAUSAGES, TOMATO SAUCE
MILK-FED CHICKEN, COMBINATION GRILL
(½ Chicken, Bacon, Tomato, Fresh Mushrooms)
BRAISED PORK TENDERLOIN, APPLE FRITTERS
ROAST PRIME RIBS OF BEEF AU JUS 3.25

•

Fresh Broccoli, Drawn Butter   Mashed Yellow Turnips
Potatoes, Rissolees

•

Corn Muffins from Carrier

•

PRR Mixed Salad

•

Freshly Baked Mince Meat Pie   Chilled Half Grapefruit   Caramel Custard, Pennsylvania
Roquefort or American Gruyere Cheese and Toasted Wafers   Baked Apple with Cream
Preserved Figs in Syrup   Chocolate or Vanilla Ice Cream, Chocolate Sauce, Cookies

Tea   Coffee   Postum   Sanka Coffee   Milk

•

Mints

The Steward of this car solicits your use
of the dining facilities for Beverage and
Refreshment Service before and after
usual hours for meals.

Food Service in Pullman space, 25c
extra per person.

TIME SAVER

Step off the train in the morning ready
to pursue the tasks or pleasures planned
for the day . . . enjoy a delicious breakfast in the diner attached to most
through over-night trains. Tell the Porter
to call you in time . . . and save time, too!

A La Carte

(When writing check please specify "a la carte")

APPETIZERS, SOUPS AND JUICES

Mixed Celery and Olives .40   Celery .30   Sliced Tomatoes .40   Olives .30
Yankee Bean Soup, Cup .35; Tureen .50   Hot Beef Broth, Cup .35
Iced Grapefruit or Tomato Juice .30

TO ORDER

Chilled Tomato Filled with Chicken Salad 1.00   Chicken Salad, Garnished 1.25
Head Lettuce Salad .50   PRR Salad Bowl, Ry-Krisp .85
Sliced Chicken Sandwich, Garnished .90   Omelet: Plain .80; with Diced Ham .95
Select Oysters au Gratin .60
Vegetable Plate, Poached Egg, Hashed in Cream Potatoes 1.25   Broiled Ham with Fried Eggs 1.25
Oven Baked Beans with Ham and Boston Brown Bread .90
Sirloin Steak from the Charcoal Grill 3.00
(With Complete Dinner $4.00)
Potatoes, Rissolees .30   Fresh Vegetables .40

BREAD

White, Whole Wheat, Rye or French Bread .15

DESSERTS AND CHEESE

Baked Apple with Cream .40   Vanilla or Chocolate Ice Cream, Sweet Cookies .35
Preserved Figs in Syrup .45   American Gruyere or Roquefort Cheese with Toasted Wafers .40
Freshly Baked Mince Meat Pie .30   Chilled Melon in Season .40
Caramel Custard, Pennsylvania .35   Vanilla Ice Cream, Chocolate Sauce .35

BEVERAGES

Tea, Coffee, Postum, Chocolate, Sanka Coffee: Pot for One .30   Milk - Individual .20

FOR THE CHILDREN . . . Parents may share their portions with Children without extra charge or half portion served at half price
to Children under ten years of age.

We shall he glad to have you mention any unusual service or attention on the part of employees. This enables us to recognize the
exceptional efficiency we wish to encourage in our service.

JOHN F. FINNEGAN, General Superintendent, Dining Car Service, Pennsylvania Railroad, Long Island City 1, N. Y.

29-11-2-48

Dinner on the Broadway Lim-
*ited was an event. It wasn't
just a meal—it was dining.
You'd want to start with a
cocktail, perhaps a Martini,
then proceed to hors d'oeuvres, then soup or chilled
tomato juice, maybe a main
course of roast prime rib of
beef au jus with fresh broccoli, mashed yellow turnips,
potatoes, corn muffins, mixed
salad, a large selection of
desserts such as caramel custard or baked apples with
cream, then coffee or tea and
mints. The dinner price:
$3.25 without the cocktail.*

TOP, LEFT. Pennyslvania Railroad trackage blanketed the East from New York to Chicago and St. Louis. It was especially prominent in Pennylvania. Here one of its many passenger trains departs Chicago. Owen Leander TOP, RIGHT. The Mountain View on the rear end of the Broadway Limited at Chicago's Union Station in February of l966. The car was retired in l968 and sold to the High Iron Company. Today the car belongs to the Railroad Museum of Pennsylvania. Charles Zeiler LEFT. By 1964, when this photo was taken, Pennsylvania passenger traffic was down, prompting the railroad to cut the service and maintenance level of its passenger trains. But the color scheme was still great! Owen Leander

ABOVE. Here's the grand Broadway Limited *leaving Chicago's Union Station, headed by three diesel units and pulling a dozen passenger cars in the classic tuscan red color. Another rail adventure has started... RIGHT. To help reduce time and cost from train movements, the Pennsylvania Railroad installed an inductive trainphone system which allowed train crews to communicate between trains and stations. Antennas were installed on the roofs of locomotives to facilitate train signals. Ken Charlton*

ABOVE. In the later years, most passenger runs were "trimmed," like this CB&Q one-diesel, four-car train shown gliding along the Mississippi River; at least there were still three dome cars. Russ Porter. LEFT. Here in Chicago the observation car Silver Crescent brings up the rear of the California Zephyr in 1969. The Budd-built car, No. 881, was a bedroom-buffet-obs and part of an order of 24 cars, all starting with the word "Silver" in their names.

RIGHT. *Towns along the line of the* California Zephyr *wanted to be a part of the CZ experience, so postcards such as this from Galesburg were printed.* BELOW. *There's No Vacation Like a Western Vacation—You may sail the Seven Seas, search the far corners of the earth...but nowhere will you find a vacationland that offers such an infinite variety of adventure, thrills, contrasts, scenic magnificence...as in Our Own West.—Burlington travel brochure courtesy Jay Chrisopher*

California Zephyr—Burlington Route
Galesburg, Illinois

Everywhere West

Way of the Zephyrs
AND VISTA-DOMES

From diesel prow to the illuminated neon *CZ* tail sign showing the twin spires of the Golden Gate Bridge, this train was meant for pleasure. The first of the three vista-dome coaches had its forward section reserved for women and children. Changing tables and bottle warmers were thoughtfully provided. Coordinated pastel colors and stainless steel trim offset the reclining leg rest seats, carpeting and venetian blinds throughout the coach section.

Bottles of a different type were found in the vista-dome buffet-lounge, which seated 19 in the main floor lounge. Its focal point was a wall-sized hand-carved linoleum map of the *CZ* route between Chicago and Oakland. The dome area was reserved for first class passengers.

Next came the sleepers, including until 1962 a stainless steel 16-section sleeper which was ultimately converted to a coach. The new 10-6 sleepers were some of the first to have the cutaway bed design, so that roomette passengers did not need to back into the aisle when raising or lowering the bed.

Perhaps the high point of *CZ* service was found in the dining car. The 48-seat diner was partitioned into semi-private nooks with etched glass panels, complemented with light green carpeting, and rose colored leather covered chairs. For years, the diner was renowned for its Colorado Rocky Mountain trout.

The lounge-observation contained three double bedrooms and a drawing room. The drawing room contained a shower, placing the *CZ* in the ranks of the *Super Chief, Century* and *Broadway Limited*. For mere mortals, the intimate lounge under the dome, or the rear observation lounge were special enough. Again, murals, deep pile carpeting and leather upholstery combined with total color coordination was the hallmark of this magnificent train.

Designed to leisurely roll through some of the most magnificent scenery in North America, what the *CZ* lacked in speed, it made up for in relaxing travel. For over a decade, that was enough.

Unfortunately, scenery and bountiful promotion could not outweigh economics. After a bitter and very public battle with the ICC for several years, the *CZ* in its original form died—with class to the end—on March 22, 1970 at the age of 21.

The CZ tail sign, which was always lighted, displayed San Francisco's Golden Gate Bridge between the train's name. The huge tail light atop the car warned trains from behind. This observation car was delivered by Budd Company in late 1948. Budd

However, in death it helped form the National Railroad Passenger Association, and its memory still lives on. Indeed, in tacit acknowledgement of the most democratic and perhaps most fondly remembered of the great postwar Western streamliners, Amtrak in 1983 renamed the Western Superliner *San Francisco Zephyr* as the *California Zephyr*. The *CZ* is dead...long live the *CZ*!

GRAND NEW TRAIN, GRAND OLD NAME: SOUTHERN'S *CRESCENT* AND SIBLINGS

Back in 1946 the Southern, Louisville & Nashville and West Point Route had placed a joint $11.5 million order for 141 streamlined cars. When delivered, these cars re-equipped the streamlined *Tennessean* and *Southerner* and created the *Royal Palm* and all-Pullman *Crescent*.

Finally, by the early fall of 1949, enough cars were delivered to inaugurate new streamliner service. Of course, both the *Tennessean* and *Southerner* had been prewar streamliners, but their

Better trains follow General Motors locomotives was the slogan used in this Electro-Motive advertisement in the Saturday Evening Post. The ad shows diesels used from all three cooperating California Zephyr *railroads: Burlington, Rio Grande and Western Pacific. Dick Bowers*

GONE are the "good old days" when a fleeting view of the glories of nature *en route* might be had through clouds of steam and smoke that streamed from the engine up ahead. All accompanied by bone-shaking jerks and jolts at stopping and starting, to say nothing of dirty hands, dirty linen and an occasional cinder in the eye.

* * *

HERE now are the grand new days with such magnificent trains as these *California Zephyrs*. They are operated jointly between Chicago and San Francisco by the Burlington, the Denver & Rio Grande Western, and the Western Pacific. Vista Dome observation affords full, free vision of the scenery amid comfortable and luxurious surroundings. These crack trains are powered by General Motors Diesel locomotives.

"Better trains follow General Motors Locomotives"

To be sure of enjoying to the full the new and exciting features that modern railroad travel provides, there is just one thing to remember: Better trains follow General Motors locomotives.

Vista Dome observation permits passengers on the California Zephyrs to enjoy to the full America's beautiful and impressive western country with its gorgeous mountains and broad plains.

ELECTRO-MOTIVE DIVISION OF GENERAL MOTORS • LA GRANGE, ILL.

Home of the Diesel Locomotive

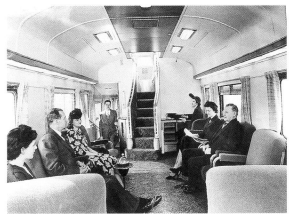

The Chicago, Burlington & Quincy Railroad, originally chartered as the Aurora Branch Railroad in February of 1849, was renamed the CB&Q in 1855. The railroad introduced the Zephyr, this country's first diesel-powered streamliner, and in 1945 the road introduced the first vista-dome cars. By 1919 the line boasted nearly 9,500 miles of trackage. Photos this page courtesy Budd, Chris Burritt, Russ Porter.

TOP, RIGHT. The Tennessean, *the diesel-powered streamliner of the Southern Railway, operated between Washington, D.C. and Memphis, Tennessee. RIGHT, BELOW. A foursome of the Pennsylvania, the Southern, the Louisville & Nashville and the West Point Route railroads teamed up to bring the streamlined* Crescent *to the traveling public as this brochure attests. "It's hard to keep an immodest pride from creeping into whatever we say or write about the Crescent," read the brochure. "Completely new from end to end, this private-room streamliner with reclining coaches available between Atlanta and New Orleans is the latest word in modern, comfortable, safe, convenient, all-weather—yes, luxurious— transportion."*

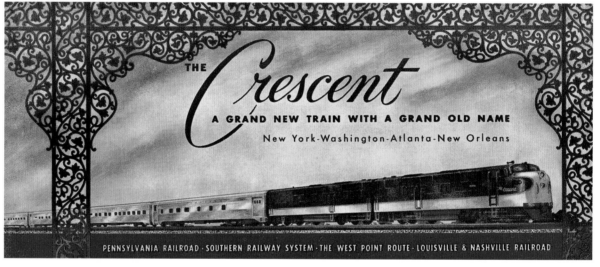

THE *Crescent*

A GRAND NEW TRAIN WITH A GRAND OLD NAME

New York-Washington-Atlanta-New Orleans

PENNSYLVANIA RAILROAD · SOUTHERN RAILWAY SYSTEM · THE WEST POINT ROUTE · LOUISVILLE & NASHVILLE RAILROAD

ABOVE AND RIGHT. The atmosphere of the Crescent's *buffet lounge car was club-like and friendly as it rolled between New York and New Orleans, through an area rich in history and tradition.*

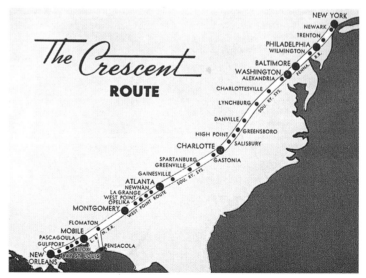

The Crescent
ROUTE

NEW YORK
NEWARK
TRENTON
PHILADELPHIA
WILMINGTON
BALTIMORE
WASHINGTON
ALEXANDRIA
CHARLOTTESVILLE
LYNCHBURG
DANVILLE
HIGH POINT   GREENSBORO
SALISBURY
CHARLOTTE
SPARTANBURG   GASTONIA
GREENVILLE
GAINESVILLE
ATLANTA
NEWNAN
LA GRANGE
WEST POINT
OPELIKA
MONTGOMERY
FLOMATON
MOBILE
PASCAGOULA
GULFPORT
BILOXI   PENSACOLA
BAY ST. LOUIS
NEW
ORLEANS

cars were in need of refurbishing or replacement. Any sleepers found in those trains during WWII almost certainly were standard Pullmans.

The *Crescent* and her siblings luxuriated in new coaches, sleepers, buffet-lounge, dining and lounge-observation cars. Most equipment was from Pullman-Standard, but Budd built the 44-seat diners, and it and ACF supplied a number of coaches.

The pinnacle of all-Pullman *Crescent* perfection was found in the master bedroom aboard the bedroom-buffet-lounge car. It was the only equipment traversing the deep South to contain a private shower. To continue in the grand manner, the lounge-observation cars had a raised Lookout Lounge, similar to those on the *20th Century Limited.*

Pastel colors, reclining seats with foot rests, comfortable Pullmans and impeccable service were the hallmarks of Southern's finest trains. As for dinner in the diner, certainly nothing was finer than the *Crescent's* prime rib, particularly after a bourbon in the *Crescent Shores* lounge.

For two decades, the streamliners continued in service. In 1955 and 1956 the *Crescent* carried transcontinental sleepers in conjunction with the Espee's *Sunset.* It took four days and three nights to cover the 3,200 miles between Washington D.C. and Los Angeles.

The *Tennessean* and *Royal Palm* were discontinued in the 1960s, but the *Crescent* and *Southerner* carried on. In 1970 the two trains were

combined and renamed the *Southern Crescent.* As Amtrak swallowed most of America's remaining passenger trains in 1971, the *Southern Crescent* remained a beacon marking a time past. For

TOP, RIGHT. A Southern Railway diesel is sandwiched in between two other roads' locomotives in this 1965 scene in Washington, D.C. The bottom headlight has been capped. BOTTOM, LEFT. No finer train to Florida than the New Royal Palm, *says the March 4, 1951 Southern timetable. The train featured reclining seat coaches, sleeping cars, a tavern-lounge, dining car service and a hostess. The daily train, which ran over three rail lines, left Chicago at 11:45 p.m. and arrived in Miami at 11:25 a.m. the second morning. BOTTOM, RIGHT. The Southern's timetable was flashy, printed in black with yellow lettering and a photograph of the* Southerner *in the center.*

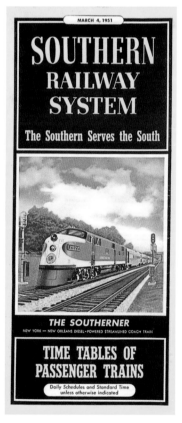

eight years the silvery streamliner showed Southern's face to the world, making lots of friends and losing lots of money in the process. Finally, New York to New Orleans service was passed to Amtrak on January 31, 1979. Southern hospitality truly was diminished.

THE LADY IN WHITE, ON THE ROAD OF ANTHRACITE, LACKAWANNA'S *PHOEBE SNOW*

On November 15, 1949 the final postwar era streamliner entered service and unknowingly

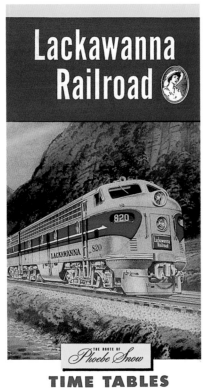

signaled the end of the massive 1946-49 expansion of service. That Eastern streamliner was the *Phoebe Snow,* and the road, the Delaware, Lackawanna & Western, sometimes irreverently called the Delay, Linger and Wait.

Miss Phoebe was the reincarnation of a 1910-era maiden dressed in white, whose clothing always remained spotless, thanks to the clean burning properties of Lackawanna anthracite coal. WWI had originally ended her career.

©1991

160

The Seaboard's Silver Meteor, *courtesy Dean Belowich*

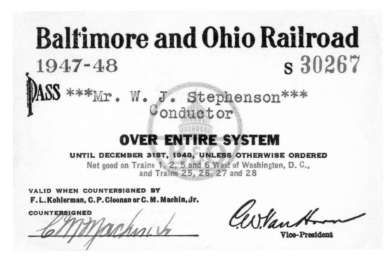

Baltimore and Ohio Railroad

1947-48   s 30267

PASS ***Mr. W. J. Stephenson***
Conductor

OVER ENTIRE SYSTEM

UNTIL DECEMBER 31ST, 1948, UNLESS OTHERWISE ORDERED
Not good on Trains 1, 2, 5 and 6 West of Washington, D. C.,
and Trains 25, 26, 27 and 28

VALID WHEN COUNTERSIGNED BY
F. L. Kohlerman, C. P. Cloonan or C. M. Machin, Jr.

COUNTERSIGNED

C. M. Machin Jr.   _G. W. Van Horn_
                                        Vice-President

*The years 1947-1948 were years of improvement and
change on U.S. railroads. Great Northern's Empire Builder
was completely re-equipped, Santa Fe ordered 27 sleepers
from Budd and 28 more from American Car & Foundry,
and Atlantic Coast Line received 30 new passenger cars.
Train travel was the way to go.*

*An unusual Baltimore & Ohio front-end diesel paint scheme
represented a trend to create less costly designs.*

Reincarnated to name the new Lackawanna streamliner between Hoboken, New Jersey and Buffalo, the grey and maroon streamliner was headed by a matched A-B-A set of EMD F-3 diesels. Behind the baggage-mail car were five streamlined coaches delivered by Pullman-Standard and American Car & Foundry. Their interior colors were various pastels, and they sported seats with foot rests.

The Budd Company provided a 36-seat diner, and ACF a couple of 10-6 sleepers. The sleepers were standard postwar stock, but the diner was first rate. With indirect lighting, white linen and china emblazoned with *Phoebe's* image, dinner was pleasantly served. No one would confuse this diner with a Manhattan supper club, but the meals were reasonable, hearty and just plain good.

Truly, Miss Phoebe saved her best for last. The rear car was a flat-end tavern-observation from Budd. The front end featured a tavern, separated from the rest of the car by a glass partition engraved with Miss Phoebe's image. It was well stocked, frequently crowded, and one's drink could be taken to a vacant chair in the observation. Phoebe's reputation for a quality drink, like her dress, was never soiled.

The *Phoebe Snow* covered the 396 miles between Hoboken and Buffalo in eight hours and 15 minutes. The daylight run transferred coaches and sleepers to the Nickel Plate Road for Chicago service.

No competition for the *Century* or *Broadway,* the *Phoebe Snow* served its New York State southern tier clientele well. New E-8 passenger locomotives soon replaced the F-3s, and for a decade the train rolled on. Unfortunately, travellers abandoned *Phoebe* for the airliner and interstate, and her last run was on Thanksgiving weekend, 1966. The workingman's streamliner passed on.

With *Phoebe Snow* came the end of the immediate postwar era of streamliner growth and expansion. Noontide was past, and the biblical injunction, "Work, for the night is coming" was upon the railroad passenger industry. For the next decade, final innovations and a slow strategic retreat from East to West was the order of the day.

Chapter Two 1950-1959
Their Noontide Passes

As the postwar '40s faded into the Fabulous '50s the Streamliner Era reached its zenith. A lengthening shadow of decline first became noticeable on the East Coast, where by the Korean War appreciable patronage had already deserted the new trains.

Enticed by the speed of the DC-7 and Lockheed Electra, or the convenience of the automobile on the new freeways and toll roads, patronage loss was significant enough that only two new Eastern streamliners were added after 1950. The Western roads had another half decade before they began feeling similar effects.

B&O'S PATRIOTIC PATRIARCH:
THE *CAPITOL LIMITED*

With a pedigree harking back to May, 1923 the all-Pullman *Capitol Limited* between Washington D.C. and Chicago was streamlined in 1950. Resplendent in Pullman stainless steel sheathing and highlighted with cream and blue paint, the *Capitol Limited* was B&O's challenge to the Pennsy's *Washington Broadway Limited*. It had been B&O's premier service since inauguration. In 1932 the *Capitol Limited* received some of the first air conditioning equipment built for regular service and in 1937 was assigned the first diesels to power an East Coast to Chicago train.

Although never as massive an operation in Washington as the Pennsylvania, still the B&O was innovative, and had a loyal cadre of patrons. The *Capitol Limited* carried not only a twin-unit diner, but along with its sister *Columbian*, the only dome car service to connect with an East Coast city north of Miami, Florida. Patrons were kept from the dome itself until past the station throat, on the off chance something should happen and the PRR catenary hit the dome roof with electrifying consequences. It never happened, and *Capitol* riders enjoyed dome amenities from the mid-1950s through the mid-1960s.

The *Capitol* proudly continued as an all-Pull-

A four-unit diesel-powered passenger train prepares to leave Chicago's Grand Central Station. The B&O at this time ran the Capitol *and* Diplomat *between Chicago and Baltimore, the* George Washington *between St. Louis and Baltimore and the* Capitol-Detroit *between Detriot and Baltimore. Owen Leander*

Strata Club *car #5551 was an 85-foot-long steel streamlined dome-coach with a capacity of 83 passengers. It had a sister, #5550. The floodlights atop the car illuminated the countryside at night so passengers could see. Owen Leander*

163

No Need to "LUG" Your Luggage on the B&O!

SELF - SERVICE

LUGGAGE CARTS

Available **Free of Charge**
at Stations in
Baltimore, Washington, Pittsburgh,
Chicago, Cincinnati, St. Louis

NEW YORK · PHILADELPHIA · BALTIMORE
WASHINGTON · PITTSBURGH · CHICAGO

The CAPITOL LIMITED

Diesel-Electric—All Pullman with Strata-Dome west of Washington

A wide choice of sleeping accommodations. Roomettes, Double Bedrooms, Compartments, Drawing Rooms, Sections. Comfortable Lounges and Observation Lounge Cars. Train Secretary.

WESTWARD (Read down)	STANDARD TIME	EASTWARD (Read up)
12.05 PM	Lv. New York (42nd St. Sta.)	Ar. 2.10 PM
2.34 PM	Lv. Philadelphia	Ar. 11.41 AM
4.18 PM	Lv. Baltimore	Ar. 9.53 AM
5.30 PM	Lv. Washington (Union Sta.)	Ar. 8.55 AM
12.10 AM	Lv. Pittsburgh (P. & L. E. Sta.)	Lv. 2.05 AM
8.00 AM	Ar. Chicago (Grand Cent. Sta.)	Lv. 4.30 PM

WASHINGTON · PITTSBURGH · CHICAGO
Through Service to and from
NEW YORK · PHILADELPHIA · BALTIMORE

The NEW COLUMBIAN

Diesel-Electric—Strata-Dome Coach Streamliner

Deluxe coaches with "Sleepy Hollow" Reclining Seats (may be reserved in advance without charge); Coffee Shoppe Car, Observation Lounge Car. Stewardess.

WESTWARD (Read down)	STANDARD TIME	EASTWARD (Read up)
12.05 PM	Lv. New York (42nd St. Sta.)	Ar. 2.10 PM
2.34 PM	Lv. Philadelphia	Ar. 11.41 AM
4.18 PM	Lv. Baltimore	Ar. 9.53 AM
5.40 PM	Lv. Washington (Union Sta.)	Ar. 8.40 AM
12.30 AM	Lv. Pittsburgh (P. & L. E. Sta.)	Lv. 1.50 AM
8.20 AM	Ar. Chicago (Grand Cent. Sta.)	Lv. 4.00 PM

BALTIMORE · WASHINGTON · PITTSBURGH
AKRON · TOLEDO · DETROIT

The AMBASSADOR

Diesel-Electric—Pullman and Coach

Modern sleepers offer a choice of Roomettes, Double and Single Bedrooms, Compartments or Sections. Reclining Seat Coach and Lounge Car.

WESTWARD (Read down)	STANDARD TIME	EASTWARD (Read up)
4.45 PM	Lv. Baltimore (Camden Sta.)	Ar. 9.20 AM
5.50 PM	Lv. Washington (Union Sta.)	Ar. 8.20 AM
12.51 AM	Ar. Pittsburgh (P. & L. E. Sta.)	Lv. 1.10 AM
3.10 AM	Ar. Akron (Union Sta.)	Lv. 10.20 PM
6.30 AM	Ar. Toledo (Union Sta.)	Lv. 7.05 PM
7.50 AM	Ar. Detroit (Mich. Cent. Sta.)	Lv. 5.45 PM

Connections Via New York Central, to and from Ann Arbor, Jackson, Battle Creek, Kalamazoo, Niles, Saginaw and Bay City.

NEW YORK · PHILADELPHIA · BALTIMORE
WASHINGTON · PITTSBURGH · CHICAGO

The SHENANDOAH

**Diesel-Electric—Pullman and Coach
Strata-Dome west of Washington***

Comfortable sleepers with Compartments, Drawing Rooms and Sections. Reclining Seat Coach—Lounge. Stewardess.

WESTWARD (Read down)	STANDARD TIME	EASTWARD (Read up)
6.15 PM	Lv. New York (42nd St. Sta.)	Ar. 9.50 PM
8.42 PM	Lv. Philadelphia	Ar. 7.26 PM
10.22 PM	Lv. Baltimore	Ar. 5.38 PM
11.40 PM	Lv. Washington	Ar. 4.30 PM
7.10 AM	Ar. Pittsburgh (P. & L. E. Sta.)	Lv. 9.10 AM
9.43 AM	Ar. Akron (Union Sta.)	Lv. 6.20 AM
3.25 PM	Ar. Chicago (Grand Cent. Sta.)	Lv. 11.00 AM

*Strata-Dome Car operates on The Shenandoah Westbound on odd dates, Eastbound on even dates. Available to Pullman Passengers only.

The Pennsylvania Railroad took advantage of its Washington, D.C. connection by using passenger train names that included "Congressional" and "Senator." The railroad also boasted of its trackwork, which was well-maintained, and often included three or even four parallel tracks. Even by 1960, the Pennsylvania owned hundreds of passenger cars such as coffee shop cars, coaches, observations, postal storage, cafe-club cars, dining cars, combines, sleepers, parlors and express cars.

Announcing Three PRR Luxury Trains

All-New Through and Through

THE MORNING CONGRESSIONAL	THE SENATOR	THE AFTERNOON CONGRESSIONAL
Washington • New York	*Washington • New York • Boston*	*Washington • New York*

America's Most Beautiful Daylight Trains

Reflecting the latest in styling, design and technological improvements, these gleaming new Pennsylvania Railroad trains are the finest ever developed for your daytime travel pleasure. Operating over the finest roadbed in the world—they serve the largest and most important cities in the East.

Accommodations for both Coach and Parlor Car passengers are of rich quality for the mood of the moment . . . to work . . . or relax . . . or dine as you travel. In addition to the restful facilities pictured here, there are handsomely furnished lounge cars with newest features for leisure and ease.

The clean, quiet atmosphere of latest-type air-conditioning . . . colorful decor . . . fluorescent lighting . . . panoramic windows . . . electro-pneumatic doors . . . enclosed telephone rooms—all these, and more, sum up to provide the most satisfactory trip you've ever taken by rail.

Enjoy the fine daily service offered by these three great streamliners. It will be a pleasant NEW experience!

NEW COACHES are roomy . . . with deeply upholstered *reclining* seats . . . plenty of baggage space. *Separate smoking compartment with 14 comfortable lounge chairs.* Complete washroom facilities.

NEW PARLOR CARS with soft-cushioned reclining swivel chairs, deep-piled carpeting, attractive draperies, ample luggage space, wide package racks. Private Drawing Room with enclosed toilet annex.

NEW DRAWING ROOM PARLOR CAR on *The Congressionals.* Private rooms with divans, lounge chairs, wardrobes. Removable partitions permit use en suite. Enclosed toilet annexes.

NEW COFFEE SHOP CAR for Coach passengers. Complete meals or snacks prepared on electric Radarange and electric grill. Served at counter or tables. Separate section with lounge facilities.

NEW DINING CARS with all-electric kitchens designed for more efficient cooking. Wonderful service in a setting of charm comparable to fine hotel facilities.

PENNSYLVANIA RAILROAD

Go by Train . . . Safety—with Speed and Comfort

165

This New York-bound train is headed by a GG-1 in Brunswick green with yellow stripes and lettering. The locomotive's geometrically perfect symmetry was designed by Raymond Loewy; the GG-1s were introduced in 1934. Russ Porter

man train until the early 1960s, and then was combined with the *Columbian*. Shorn of its dining car and most of its sleepers, the *Capitol Limited* was a shadow of its former self when eternity overtook it on Amtrak Day. Still, the name lives on, with Amtrak's reincarnation of Chicago-Washington service via CSX.

PENNSY'S PRIDE: THE NEW
CONGRESSIONAL

Master of the yet-to-be-named Northeast Corridor, the Pennsylvania remained a railroad barony in 1950. Still powerful, superbly-financed and well-connected in the postwar years, Pennsy took seriously its self-proclaimed moniker: The Standard Railroad of the World. Long haul passenger service might be symbolized by the impeccable *Broadway Limited*, but the high-density racetrack between New York City and Washington D. C. was another story. In that marketplace, the *Congressional* was first among equals.

Thus, in 1950 the Pennsy placed orders with Budd totalling 64 cars to supply four new train-

166

sets. Two 18-car *Congressional* and 14-car *Senator* sets were the result. The *Senator* set covered a single daily roundtrip between Washington D.C. and Boston while the *Morning* and *Afternoon Congressional* sets each made a daily roundtrip between New York City and Washington.

The *Morning* and *Afternoon Congressional* sets were the longest matched consists ever ordered and placed in service in North America, perhaps in the world. Reflecting the circles of business, government and financial power, each *Congressional* carried five parlor cars, one parlor-conference and a twin-unit diner. Overflow from the diner was handled by the coffee-shop-tavern.

ABOVE. GG-1 #4938 with huge Pennsylvania red and white logo on the side sits at Washington, D.C. in October of 1958 awaiting clearance. As of April, 1966, Pennsy still rostered GG-ls #4800-4803 and #4805-4826 on the Harrisburg Division and #4827-4830, #4832-4846 and #4848-4938 on the New York Division.

Pennsylvania Timetable of June 30, 1952 lists some of its trains, stations and running times between New York City and Pittsburgh.

New York, Philadelphia, Washington and Baltimore to Pittsburgh—(Continued on Page 13)

Miles	Table 1 (For additional stops consult local time tables. For Sleeping, Parlor, Dining Cars and Coaches, see pages 4 and 5) (Eastern Standard Time)	Mail and Express 13-85 Sunday only	Mail and Express 13 Except Sunday	The Metropolitan 25 Daily	Mail and Express 205-19 Except Sunday	The Duquesne 75 Daily	The St. Louisan 33 Daily	Manhattan Limited 23 Daily	The General 49 Daily	The Trail Blazer 49 Daily	Liberty Limited 59 Daily	Broadway Limited 29 Daily	"Spirit of St. Louis" 31 Daily
		AM	AM	AM	AM	AM	PM	PM	PM	PM	PM	PM	PM
.0	Lv New York, N.Y. (Penna. Sta.)	2.45	2.45	7.05	y 8.00	v10.45	v12.55	v 1.50	z 4.00	z 4.00	------	t 5.00	v 5.10
	Lv New York, N.Y. (Hudson Term.)	2.20	2.20	6.45	y 7.48	v10.24	v12.36	v 1.36	z 3.40	z 3.40	------	t 4.48	v 4.56
	" Jersey City, N.J. (Exchange Pl.)(u)	2.23	2.23	6.48	y 7.51	v10.27	v12.39	v 1.39	z 3.43	z 3.43		t 4.51	v 4.59
	Ar Newark, N.J.	2.40	2.40	7.05	y 8.08	v10.44	v12.56	v 1.56	z 4.00	z 4.00		t 5.08	v 5.16
10.0	Lv Newark, N.J.	3.00	3.00	7.20	y 8.14	v10.59	v 1.10	v 2.05	z 4.14	z 4.14		t 5.14	v 5.25
58.1	" Trenton, N.J.	------	m 3.49	8.05	y 8.57	v11.43		v 2.49	z 4.55	z 4.55			
85.9	Philadelphia, Pa. " North Philadelphia Station	4.23	4.23	8.41		c12.13	c 2.24	c 3.20	z 5.20	z 5.20		t 6.21	c 6.40
	" Pennsylvania Station (30th St.)				10.10								
111.4	" Paoli, Pa.			9.07	10.40	12.41	2.53	3.48	z 5.45	z 5.45		t 6.46	
124.0	" Downingtown, Pa.			9.21	10.54	12.58		4.06			For Special Service Charge See Page 39.	Sleeping Cars and Reserved Seat Coaches	7.05
130.0	" Coatesville, Pa.			9.30	11.05								
135.7	" Parkesburg, Pa.				11.14								
159.3	" Lancaster, Pa.	5.47	5.47	10.00	11.45	1.27	3.37	4.35	6.27	6.27			7.48
170.8	" Mount Joy, Pa.	6.04	6.04										
177.6	" Elizabethtown, Pa.	6.19	6.19										
185.1	" Middletown, Pa.	6.31	6.31		12.13								
194.6	Ar Harrisburg, Pa.	6.45	6.45	10.35	12.28	2.01	4.10	5.08	7.02	7.02		t 8.01	8.22
.0	Lv Washington, D.C.			7.10			1.10					g 4.30	5.25
40.1	" Baltimore, Md. (Penna. Sta.)			8.03			1.56		Sleeping Cars.	Reserved Seat Coaches.		g 5.15	6.10
96.3	" York, Pa.			9.37			3.25					6.44	7.39
123.4	Ar Harrisburg, Pa.			10.25			4.05					7.25	8.20
194.6	Lv Harrisburg, Pa.	7.10	7.10	10.46	12.45	2.01	4.22	5.08	7.02	7.02		7.25	t 8.01	8.22
209.4	" Duncannon, Pa.	7.32	7.32		1.08								
222.0	" Newport, Pa.	7.46	7.46		1.29								
243.6	" Mifflin, Pa.	8.10	8.10		1.54								
255.2	" Lewistown, Pa.	8.25	8.25	11.49	2.13				6.22				
279.7	" Mount Union, Pa.	8.55	8.55		2.44				6.49				
291.6	" Huntingdon, Pa.	9.15	9.15		3.13				7.03				
311.2	" Tyrone, Pa.	9.55	9.55	12.50	3.58	4.10			7.30				
325.4	Ar Altoona, Pa.	10.30	10.30	1.16	4.45	4.35	6.40		7.56	9.25	9.25	9.48	10.50
325.4	Lv Altoona, Pa.	10.50	10.50	1.16	5.05	4.35	6.40		7.56	9.25	9.25	9.48	10.50
339.9	" Cresson, Pa.	11.24	11.26		5.42				9.00				
362.9	" Johnstown, Pa.	11.57	12.15	2.18	6.58	5.37							
387.0	" Torrance, Pa.		x12.55		7.37								
394.3	" Derry, Pa.				7.47								
399.2	" Latrobe, Pa.	12.40	1.23		8.02	6.16			9.41				
408.5	" Greensburg, Pa.	12.57	2.02	3.07	8.45	6.29			9.55				
412.6	" Jeannette, Pa.				8.57								
417.9	" Irwin, Pa.				9.09								
425.5	" Wilmerding, Pa.				9.24								
427.1	" East Pittsburgh, Pa.				9.33							No Coaches or Checked Baggage.	No Coaches or Checked Baggage.
429.2	" Braddock, Pa.				9.44								
432.7	" Wilkinsburg, Pa.				9.51								
434.7	" East Liberty, Pa.	1.34	3.02	3.43		7.04		10.32					
439.3	Ar Pittsburgh, Pa.	1.45	3.15	3.55	10.05	7.15	9.10	10.43	11.54	11.54		12.17	12.52	1.19
		PM	PM	PM	PM	PM	PM	PM	PM	PM		AM	AM	AM

167

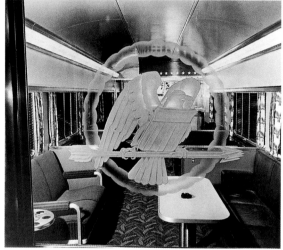

No postwar streamliner had more parlor car or drawing room accommodations available, with the possible exception of the New Haven's *Merchants Limited.* However, it was not ordered as a single operating consist.

The *Senator* sets were not quite so opulent, but certainly weren't second class in anybody's book. In each direction they handled eight coaches, one coffee-shop-tavern, one full diner, three parlors and a parlor-observation.

All the Budd equipment was fluted stainless steel, with a tuscan red letterboard carrying "Pennsylvania" centered across the carbody. The cars were all single vestibule-equipped, except for the diners, which had none. Still rare for the times, each *Senator* and *Congressional* set had radio-telephone service available.

Car interiors featured patriotic red, white and blue color themes in various combinations. The 60-seat coaches had linoleum tile covering the floors, while antimacassars covered each seat-back. The parlor cars were carpeted in either a rose and grey combination cornucopia or blue feather pattern. Etched scenes on all the glass bulkheads in the cars depicted various historical events. The observation-lounge and dining cars had venetian blinds and all the comforts of 1950s civilized society.

On March 17, 1952 inaugural *Congressional* and *Senator* service departed Washington, New York and Boston respectively, and Pennsy's last great effort in the passenger business began. For the next 15 years, the *Afternoon Congressional* was the fastest thing on wheels between New York and Washington, rolling behind its specially painted GG-1 electric at up to 110 mph for a carded time of three hours, 35 minutes between end points.

After only four years of glory, both *Congressional* and *Senator* began to change, initially impacted by the loss of first class patronage to the airlines. The development of the jetliner only exacerbated the traffic loss by the 1960s. Onward each *Congressional* and *Senator* continued—still behind GG-1s approaching 40 years of age—through and long past 1971s Amtrak Day. Indeed, even today a significant number of those 1952 Budd-built *Congressional* and *Senator* cars continue to haul patrons—admittedly commuters—nearly 50 years later. The spirits of Edward G. Budd and William W. Atterbury still rest in peace.

DOMES UNDER WIRES FOR THE *SNOWBIRDS*

Alongside the posh and fancy *Congressionals* and *Senators,* the mighty PRR continued to handle Florida trains for the Seaboard, ACL and

FEC. Popular for over two generations, the only item these streamliners seemed to lack was the dome car. Unfortunately, domes could not fit safely through the tight tunnels and under the looping catenary of the Northeast Corridor.

On January 24, 1956 Pullman-Standard rolled out Sun Lounge sleeper *Hollywood Beach* for its new owner, Seaboard Air Line. Fabricated of Cor-Ten steel with stainless steel fluting, it was of typical P-S construction. However, the 13 1/2-foot-high car had a lounge with skylights therein: the Sun Lounge. It was just the place for 21 cold but convivial Northeast snowbirds to warm up on a

long-anticipated trip to the Florida sun.

Interior decor consisted of thick carpet carrying a seashell pattern, driftwood-based lamps and colorful tropical murals. The buffet beckoned with drinks more warming and potent than just Florida orange juice, and soon all manner of iciness melted away. Huge 42" x 58" windows let in any available sunlight, and curved panes on each side of the ceiling opened nearly half of the square footage of the roof line to daylight. It was sunny, even on a cloudy day. Five double bedrooms completed the car's interior.

The three cars: *Hollywood Beach, Miami*

ABOVE, TOP. Pennsy's AeroTrain, introduced in 1956, was predicated on the idea of a novel suspension system that made use of compressed air in rubber bellows rather than metal springs. Built by General Motors, the low, sleek stream-lined train was labeled "experimental" by the railroad. It ran briefly between Pittsburgh and New York on a daily basis. EMD FAR LEFT. A number of railroads—including the Pennsylvania—made connections with other railroads to transport passengers from the colder northern cities to Florida. The Pennsy cooperated with the Seaboard Air Line, the Atlantic Coast Line, the Norfolk & Western and the Southern. A New York-bound train from Florida pulls out of the station. Russ Porter. RIGHT. Seaboard Coast Line's Silver Star (Trains 21-121) was a Boston to Tampa (and beyond) train that featured reclining seats, a tavern-observation-lounge, dining car and sleepers—plus a registered nurse. Owen Leander

Interior of Atlantic Coast Line passenger cars—a dome and a chair car—show the state-of-the-art in 1947 of the American passenger train. Improvements in carpeting, draperies and lighting were part of the new creature comforts. Both photos, Budd

A typical Seaboard Air Line diner crew assigned to the all-Pullman Boston/New York to Miami Orange Blossom Special *consisted of a steward, four cooks and seven waiters. The train ran over the Seaboard; Richmond, Fredericksburg & Potomac; Pennsylvania; and New Haven.*

Beach and *Palm Beach*, were promptly assigned to the *Silver Meteor* where they remained until well into the Amtrak era. In the late 1970s the three distinctive cars passed into private hands and all are preserved.

Still, the most important milestone these cars marked was as the final new sleeping car design of the Streamliner Era to be built by Pullman-Standard. An era that started with the all-aluminium

TOP. Seaboard's Silver Meteor (Train #58) with fluted-side cars, zips down the track leaving Ft. Lauderdale, Florida toward its destination in this December 24, 1969 scene. The train had reserved coach seating only. Lou O'Brien BOTTOM. With three diesel units in the lead, the Seaboard's Silver Meteor arrives at Ft. Lauderdale in December of 1968. The train was inaugurated in February of 1939 and was an all-coach Budd-built fleet of stainless steel cars. The railroad at one point added a glass-roofed car in lieu of dome cars which could not be handled because of clearances in the East. Lou O'Brien

Diesel locomotives built by Electro-Motive Division of General Motors are in use on the PENNSYLVANIA RAILROAD.

TEXAS AND PACIFIC RAILWAY COMPANY, route of the Sunshine Special and the Texan, will use starting early this year Diesel locomotives built by Electro-Motive Division of General Motors.

WABASH RAILROAD COMPANY provides fast, comfortable passenger train service through the "Heart of America". The "Follow the Flag" route uses Diesel locomotives built by Electro-Motive Division of General Motors.

One of NORTHERN PACIFIC RAILWAY'S 4500 H.P. Diesel passenger locomotives built by Electro-Motive Division of General Motors.

The wide range F3 General Motors Diesel locomotive built by Electro-Motive Division. The basic F3 can be equipped to cover services ranging from the heaviest duty freight to hundred mile an hour heavy duty passenger.

The American postwar streamliner era was exciting and colorful, with each railroad vying to outdo one another in passenger convenience and comfort. The detailed painting/lettering schemes of the diesels and car consists alone is worth a sustained look: from Brunswick green to purples and yellows, to reds, maroons and oranges, the lines carried their colors over as well to logos, stationary, menus, napkins, brochures, timetables, tickets and baggage tags. The year 1945 saw 2,993 passenger cars ordered from builders, the fourth largest number ordered since 1898: the postwar travel surge had begun. EMD

A fleet of powerful Diesel freight locomotives, built by Electro-Motive Division of General Motors, helps give dependable, efficient, economical freight transportation service on the 8,000-mile SOUTHERN RAILWAY SYSTEM that "Serves the South."

Diesel locomotives built by Electro-Motive Division of General Motors are in use on the PENNSYLVANIA RAILROAD.

SEABOARD AIR LINE RAILROAD serves ports and capitals of six southeastern states. Its all-Pullman Orange Blossom Special, Florida Sunbeam, streamlined Silver Meteors and fast freight trains use Diesel locomotives built by Electro-Motive Division of General Motors.

SEABOARD AIR LINE RAILROAD serves ports and capitals of six southeastern states. Its all-Pullman Orange Blossom Special, Florida Sunbeam, streamlined Silver Meteors and fast freight trains use Diesel locomotives built by Electro-Motive Division of General Motors.

BALTIMORE AND OHIO RAILROAD uses Diesel locomotives built by Electro-Motive Division of General Motors to power their fleet of feature trains in fast service with on-time dependability.

RIO GRANDE RAILROAD, direct central trans-continental route through Colorado and Utah, depends on its fleet of General Motors Diesel freight locomotives, built by Electro-Motive Division of General Motors, to maintain fast freight and passenger schedules.

Diesel locomotives built by Electro-Motive Division of General Motors are among those the CENTRAL OF GEORGIA relies upon to render high quality railroad service.

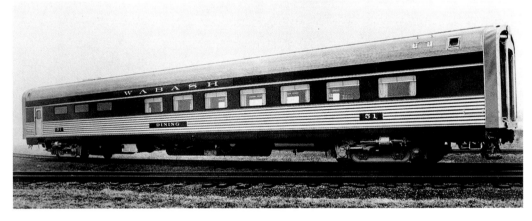

ABOVE. *"Most modern train in America"* is how the Wabash rated its 1950 six-car Budd-built Blue Bird *that ran between St. Louis and Chicago. The streamliner left St. Louis every morning and Chicago every afternoon. The train offered a Pullman parlor car with a dome, coaches with domes and a coffee shop club car. RIGHT. Wabash 85-foot-long diner-lounge car #51 had a seating capacity of 52 and was built by Budd in 1949. Budd*

George M. Pullman of 1933 ended some 23 years later with this order. Historians note its passing well. ACF would have but another decade, and Budd, until the late-1970s, before they too faded from the scene.

BLUE BIRD SINGS WABASH MELODY

Not yet afflicted with the loss of patronage appearing on Eastern streamliners, on February 26, 1950 the Wabash inaugurated a 6-car Budd-built streamliner in the hotly contested St. Louis-Chicago market. The new *Blue Bird* consisted of a baggage-buffet-lounge, three dome-coaches, diner-lounge and a dome-parlor-observation. The spiffy little train accommodated 28 parlor and drawing room patrons and 162 in coach.

Shotwelded of stainless steel, the car's window bands and letterboard were painted dark Wabash blue, as was the underbody and its equipment. Full-width diaphragms connected the cars, and power was supplied by either EMD E units or Alco PAs.

Coach passengers luxuriated in Sleepy Hollow seats, while a total of 73 non-revenue seats awaited them in three coach-domes. The 28 parlor passengers had 24 dome seats to share in the dome-parlor-observation. The diner seated 40, while its cocktail lounge accommodated 12. The lunch-

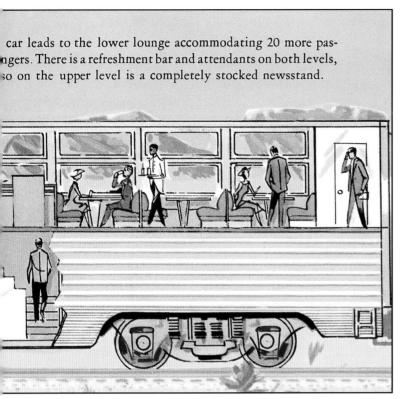

car leads to the lower lounge accommodating 20 more passengers. There is a refreshment bar and attendants on both levels, so on the upper level is a completely stocked newsstand.

final and perhaps greatest contribution to the streamliner.

Quietly, in the summer of 1954 two Hi-Level coaches departed from Budd for testing on the Santa Fe *El Capitan*. The same height and length as the Big Domes which preceded them by about six months, they broke new ground. For the first time, the entire passenger level of the train was at the nominal height of a dome car floor, or some four feet above the traditional passenger car floor. This gave passengers a smoother and quieter ride, being that much further from the rails.

Additionally, such services as restrooms and baggage storage were placed on the lower level, dropped about two feet below standard floor level, and filling the space between the trucks. The crawl space over each truck held support systems such as air conditioning, heating and brake equipment.

The public instantly approved of Santa Fe's new equipment, and in 1955 Budd received an order for 35 coaches—10 of which stepped down to regular floor level to connect with stan-

dard equipment, six lounges and six full diners. Not only were the passengers enthusiastic, but the operating and financial departments liked the new Hi-Level equipment.

Because the upper level was now devoid of operating equipment and restrooms, about 50% more passengers could be handled in the same length car. The new coaches handled either 68 or 72 patrons in comfort, excelling that found in the 44- or 48-seat coaches they replaced. Likewise, the two 33-seat lunch counter-diners were replaced with a single 80-passenger dining car complete with two dumbwaiters to the kitchen below. The lounge seated 60 in the Top of the Cap, with an additional 28 seats in the intimate Kachina Coffee Shop below. The net result was 496 patrons could now be handled in an *El Capitan* which consisted of seven coaches, one diner and one lounge. An eighth coach, two lunch-counter diners, and lounge-observation-equipped predecessor handled but 350 patrons, and weighed roughly the same. The new equipment allowed Santa Fe to haul 30% more passengers in

ABOVE, LEFT. The Santa Fe's high-level lounge car on the El Capitan, called Top of the Cap, was a luxurious car with spacious accommodations for a drink, to gather for socializing or watching the scenery. LEFT. The Southern Pacific's bright, colorful ads invited passengers to ride the new San Franciso-Portland Shasta Daylight which was pegged as a million dollar train. ABOVE, RIGHT. Southern Pacific's Sunset Limited car #9903 was an 85-foot-long sleeper. The Sunset Limited was the premier train of this southernmost line to the West Coast. Budd

greater comfort without increasing the total weight of the *El Capitan.*

With fanfare and promotion worthy of the Santa Fe, the new *Hi-Level El Capitan* entered service on July 7, 1956. Both east- and westbound sections met the following day in Albuquerque, New Mexico to assist in celebrating that city's 250th birthday. They had already drawn nation-wide attention between Santa Fe's on-line promo-tions and a number of whistle stop tours on their way from Budd in Philadelphia.

The Hi-Level cars rolled on in solitary splendor for only about 18 months before the unthinkable happened. Facing fiscal and traffic realities, on January 12, 1958 the *Super Chief* and *El Capitan* were combined into a single train for the winter season. Thus ended Santa Fe's long and impres-sive record of all-Pullman service stretching back into the 1890s. For the 13 remaining years until Amtrak, the *Super Chief* and *El Capitan* remained separate trains in the summer and holi-day seasons, but with the coach train running as the second section of the *Super Chief,* no longer under its own train number.

Although the trains were coupled together, they remained socially separate. The *Super Chief* clientele had their single level equipment in the rear of the train, while the *High Level El Capitan* had its coaches, lounge and diner up front. Except for an emergency, there was no intermin-gling of patrons.

The high level concept was so successful that as late as 1964 the Santa Fe ordered another 24 cars and placed them on the *San Francisco Chief* and later on the *Texas Chief* as well. Of course, this concept was picked up by Amtrak in the mid-1970s when it ordered 284 bi-level cars to re-equip its Western fleet. After that order arrived, only the former Santa Fe equipment remained in regular usage on Western routes. It is the ultimate tribute to Santa Fe's passenger heritage that their high level equipment lasted so long, many years after construction.

SOUTHERN PACIFIC: OBSERVATION OFF—AUTOMAT ON

The mighty Southern Pacific placed its ultimate streamliner in service on August 20, 1950. The postwar years had seen the Espee expand its streamliner fleet to include the *Owl, Lark, Starlight, Shasta Daylight, Cascade* and others, as well as its interline services with RI and UP between the West Coast and Chicago or St. Louis.

The Espee spared no expense with the re-equipping of its storied *Sunset Limited* service

between Los Angeles and New Orleans. SP Trains #1 and #2 were allotted five 15-car Budd stainless steel equipment sets which cost a total of $15 million, and were filled with dining, lounging and various sleeping accommodations. The *Sunset,* from *Daylight* red/yellow/orange painted flat-nosed Alco PA power, to the square-tailed red-striped sleeper observation with wrap-around stainless steel fluting, featured all the amenities Budd and SP could envision.

Perhaps most fondly remembered from the streamlined *Sunset* was the *French Quarter* lounge car, complete with photomurals and New Orleans decor. Lucius Beebe extolled its virtues. Not far behind was the *Pride of Texas* coffee shop lounge car, for those who did not choose to avail themselves of the full dining car.

In 1955 and 1956 the *Sunset Limited* carried through Pullmans from coast to coast. End points were Washington and Los Angeles.

Regardless of the amenities aboard, it still took 42 hours to cover the 2,069 miles between Los Angeles and New Orleans. Interline service to Washington added another 25 hours, and up to San Francisco, 12 hours. The combined approximately 70 hours from coast to coast soon paled

against the turboprop aircraft, much less the pending passenger jet.

By the mid-1950s the Espee had lost faith in the passenger train as a commercially profitable form of transportation and wanted out. Tragically, the

The Great Northern's transcontinental route was the most northern of all the U.S. lines, with the famous Empire Builder, the railroad's premier passenger train. The all-reserved train ran between Chicago and Seattle, with various connections to Tacoma, British Columbia and California. The train consisted of dome coaches, ranch-lounge (meals and beverage service), full dining car and several sleeping cars.

182

POST-WAR VACATION

this is the year and this the right train

Seattle and Portland are only two nights from Chicago on Great Northern's swift, streamlined *New Empire Builder.* No extra fare.

Modern coaches with leg rests. No additional charge for reserved seats.

You enjoy privacy and restful sleep in luxurious duplex roomettes and bedrooms.

GREAT NORTHERN'S
NEW EMPIRE BUILDER

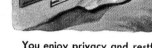

● This year visit the Pacific Northwest and California to your heart's content. Travel on the *first* and *finest* postwar transcontinental train. Diesel powered, this green and orange superliner streaks along the smoothest roadbed in the Northwest. Inside there's more color, more comfort, more convenience than you'd have thought possible before the war. Come aboard soon! Write to V. J. KENNY, Passenger Traffic Manager, Great Northern Railway, St. Paul 1, Minn.

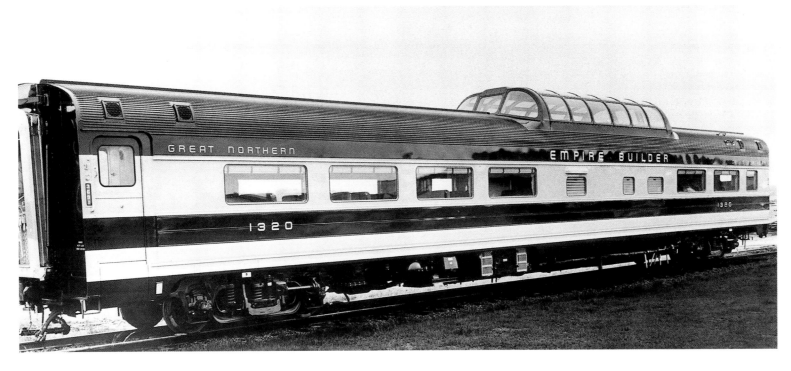

Sunset figured prominently in the Espee's battle to drop money-losing services, which culminated in the once majestic train being reduced to a single coach with a food service car carrying an automat.

Still, the *Sunset Limited* rolls on today, resuscitated by Amtrak into a full-service, Superliner-equipped train, on a tri-weekly schedule. Ironically, of the hundreds of streamlined passenger cars purchased by the Espee between 1936 and 1955, only the stainless steel *Sunset* cars are still in Amtrak service.

GN CLASSIC: THE *MID-CENTURY EMPIRE BUILDER*

Rather than order additional sleepers for the ever-popular *Empire Builder*, the Great Northern in 1949 announced it was going to replace the entire train. They placed orders with ACF and Pullman-Standard for the five, 15-car sets which would make up the new *Empire Builder*. Of the 75 total cars, 59 were owned by the GN, 14 by the Burlington and two by the SP&S.

Pullman-Standard provided the baggage-mail cars, sleepers and 48-seat coaches while ACF constructed the coffee shop-lounges, diners, observation lounges, 60-seat coaches and baggage-dormitory cars. The car order, without locomotives, totalled $12 million.

The nominal *Mid-Century Empire Builder* could accommodate 335 passengers. Each equipment set included a mail-baggage car, baggage-dormitory, 60-seat coach, three 48-seat coaches, coffee shop-lounge, diner, six sleepers and the lounge-observation.

The 1947 *Empire Builder* equipment was refurbished and became the *Western Star*, running on a slightly slower schedule than the premier *Builder*.

Perhaps the most distinctive car on the *Mid-Century Empire Builder* was the coffee shop-lounge. Entitled The Ranch, its interior decor was straight out of the Old West. Walls were finished in stained grey tongue-and-groove oak boards. Partitions between the lounge, coffee shop and dining sections were constructed of cedar log sections, debarked, polished and stained dark red. The brand or logo of the GN, G-bar-N, was displayed over the bar in the fashion of a cattleman's brand. The GN even registered the G-bar-N brand. The lounge seated 18, while the coffee shop seated 12 at tables and 14 along the lunch counter.

For contrast, the *Empire Builder's* 36-seat din-

This coach-dome was built by Budd and had a seating capacity in the observation dome of 24 with a lower level seating of 52. The striking green and orange colors of the Great Northern passenger equipment made a lengthy train stand out. Budd

RIGHT. *The* Western Star *was a daily, each way, train between Chicago and Seattle-Portland via St. Paul and Spokane. The traveler would see the Mississippi River bluffs, Glacier National Park, the Rocky Mountains and the Cascades en route. Russ Porter* BELOW. *"Travel to and through mountain wonderlands aboard this sleek streamlined train," read the advertising copy next to this picture of the* Western Star. *The train stopped daily at the eastern and western Glacier Park entrances during the summer season.*

ing car was a study in pastels. The ceiling was pale green, window pier panels were light beige and the wainscoting silver grey. The floor was carpeted in green and the chairs upholstered in rose needlepoint. The entryway partitions were of 1/2 inch thick safety glass, with etched scenes of the industry and natural resources found in the service areas of the railroad.

All coaches shared various combinations of pastel colors in ceiling, wall and floor materials. The 60-seat "shorts" coach had footrests, while the 48-seat long-haul coaches were equipped with deeply reclining leg rest seats called day-nite seating.

The observation-lounge cars carried no saleable space. Each car had two roomettes, but these were reserved for the passenger service representative and the Pullman conductor. Separating the lounge and observation areas was a glass partition with etched images of the various Western states and Canadian provinces served by the GN. It was a virtual mid-town hotel lobby lounge on wheels.

Still determined to be the best of the Northwest, when the GN learned its competition had

ordered domes as the ultimate passenger pleaser, the *Builder* would be so equipped. Lavishly.

In time for the summer, 1955 season, Budd delivered 22 domes for *Empire Builder* service: 17 to GN; four to CB&Q; and one to SP&S. Each of the five *Builder* consists had three Budd dome-coaches and a single full-length dome-lounge for first class passengers. A spare of each type was included in the $6 million order. No train in North America except the *California Zephyr* and *Twin Cities Zephyr's* regularly carried more dome cars than the *Empire Builder*.

The *Builder* rolled on throughout the 60s,

exchanging its aging EMD F units for twin 3,600-hp SD-45s and its classic orange and green paint for Big Sky blue as the decade waned. Its final color schemes was a hodgepoge, thanks to the consolidation of the CB&Q, GN, and NP into the Burlington Northern in 1970.

A veritable riot of colors, the *Builder* rolled into Amtrak in 1971, with passengers still admiring the plains, Rocky Mountains and Pacific Northwest through its sparkling dome windows. The *Empire Builder*, appropriately enough, was the first Amtrak service to receive Superliner equipment.

This 2,000-hp E-7 diesel passenger locomotive was built by EMD in 1947. The engine is at Duluth 20 years later, and doesn't have much time left before it's scrapped. Owen Leander

Another colorful streamliner was the Northern Pacific's North Coast Limited, *which used Budd's Slumbercoaches in the consist starting in the late 1950s. Other cars used on the train included Pullman sleeping cars, a dining car, reclining chair coaches, dome cars and a buffet-lounge which featured select and a la carte meals, snacks and beverages.*

NORTHERN PACIFIC'S *NORTH COAST LIMITED* CHALLENGE

Although always a slower routing than its GN competition, the Northern Pacific was not about to concede its share of the passenger business to anyone. After all, few railroads dated their charters back to Abraham Lincoln and advertised their services in 1875 as "protected by the U.S. Army!"

The streamlined *North Coast Limited* had been a rousing success since introduction piecemeal during 1947-48. Now, in 1954 the streamliner was the first in the Pacific Northwest to receive Budd dome equipment. Ten dome-coaches and 10 dome-sleepers were placed in the equipment pool that year and proved immensely popular. Of each 10 cars, NP owned seven, Burlington two and SP&S one. Most unusual were the dome-sleepers, containing four roomettes, four duplex single rooms and four double bedrooms.

As the decade continued, in 1954 the NP placed in service their famed *Louis & Clark Travellers Rest* buffet-lounge cars. Containing rustic Old West decor, the cars provided light meal and drink service in a relaxed atmosphere.

To complement the *Travellers Rest* equipment, in 1958 the NP received six new dining cars from Budd for $2 million. Pastel interiors offset with etched glass pier panels at each end of the car were highlighted by the snowy table linen and excellent meals. These cars were the last streamlined dining cars off the Budd assembly line, some 24 years after the *Pioneer Zephyr* introduced the Streamliner Era.

In its continuing effort to keep passenger traffic, in 1959 the NP placed Budd's newly-designed Slumbercoach in the consist of the *North Coast Limited*. These sleeping cars managed to hold 24 single rooms and eight double rooms in a standard car length. Always popular, they marked the end of a quarter-century of Budd passenger car innovations, and remained in Amtrak service until September 1996.

The NP turned the *North Coast Limited* over to Amtrak, which continued to operate the service until 1979. Government bureaucracy then accomplished what no competitive railroad or transportation mode could: the last run of the *North Coast Limited*. Its epitaph is written in the domes and diners still in daily Amtrak service.

ABOVE. Car #553 was a deluxe coach dome with a seating capacity of 70. The paint scheme was a striking two-tone green. Doug Wornom LEFT. The Traveller's Rest *on the NP was a buffet-lounge car where passengers could enjoy a drink and socialize. The car, whose interior was designed by Raymond Loewy, was named after a favorite campsite of Lewis and Clark .*

Burlington's *big new*

VISTA-DOME DENVER ZEPHYR

CHICAGO—DENVER—COLORADO SPRINGS

Bigger, Brighter, More Beautiful were the watchwords for the vista-dome Denver Zephyr introduced by the Burlington. The railroad advertised modern color schemes, bright floral pictures in the bedrooms, authentic Western murals and wood carvings in the Chuck Wagon diner.

OVERNIGHT, EVERY NIGHT, THE BURLINGTON'S CURTAIN CALL

As the premier promoter of stainless steel streamliners, the Burlington entered the early 1950s filled with boundless enthusiasm. The postwar *California Zephyr* was carrying capacity loads, as were virtually all the other *Zephyrs*. Expansion was still the order of the day.

With more equipment arriving from Budd as soon as the Korean War ended, the year 1953 found the inauguration of the *Kansas City Zephyr*, the *American Royal Zephyr* and the re-

VISTA-DOMES!

Plenty to see...wonderful views for all passengers
...presented by Burlington, first to offer Vista-Dome Travel

establishment of the *Ark-Sar-Ben Zephyr.* The Burlington Zephyr truly went *Everywhere West.*

The newest, and ultimately the last Budd-built streamlined train was received by the Burlington in 1956. Ordered to replace the 1936 semi-articulated *Denver Zephyr,* the new *DZ* was top drawer. Two 14-car train sets represented a $6.5 million investment by the Burlington, solid proof of the road's commitment to passenger service.

Each *Denver Zephyr* included two 2,400-hp EMD E-9 locomotives, baggage car, RPO car, two coaches, vista-dome coach, two Slumbercoaches, *Chuck Wagon* dome-buffet-lounge, 48-seat dining car, four sleepers and the vista-dome-parlor-lounge-observation.

The interiors were classic. The *Chuck Wagon* car was fitted in Old West leather and accented with copper and stainless steel. Murals and linoleum carvings adorned the various cars' bulkheads throughout the ´train. Pastel colors of brown, blue and green predominated, but all cars were color coordinated. Even the violet and daisy china in the dining car complemented the interior colors of blue, rose and warm brown.

The public responded to the new *Denver Zephyrs* wholeheartedly. Regularly sold out, dur-

ing the holiday season the train was frequently broken into Pullman and coach sections, each running 14- or 15-cars strong. Between their debut on October 28, 1956 and October 28, 1961, the *DZ* grossed $22.1 million and carried $9.1 million to the bottom line as profit.

Until the mid-60s the *Denver Zephyr* held strong patronage in its overnight market. By 1970 even the Burlington had to face change, as the mail contracts came off, and it melded itself into the new BN. The *Denver Zephyr* equipment, along with virtually all the Burlington, GN and NP's streamlined equipment, entered Amtrak service in 1971.

ABOVE, LEFT. A table setting on the Twin Cities Zephyr *was composed of heavy china and silverware.*
ABOVE, RIGHT. The Kansas City Zephyr *tailend car was called a blunt-end observation. Both photos, Budd*

189